A DISCARDED BRAT

To

Mrs Philip

With the Compliments

of the auth:

(Signed)

9th August 1889

THIS is the sixth re-print of "A Discarded Brat", proof indeed of the popularity this enthralling novel of a 'waif' has enjoyed since first hitting the book shelves.

Suzie, as she is affectionately known to a host of friends in and around Inverness, is one of the town's chief contributors to local charities and, since putting pen to paper for the first time several years ago, has accomplished two feats which would have shaken lesser, lithe mortals.

At the ripe old age of 73 she decided to climb Britain's highest mountain — Ben Nevis — taking the task in her stride and raising £2,029 in the process, money which saw the underprivileged children of the Highland capital in 1982-83 enjoy two memorable Christmas Parties in the Caledonian Hotel Ballroom.

But Suzie's hard earned cash has not only gone to help make children happy at Christmas time. A host of local charities have benefitted from her efforts including £1,000 to the local Scanner Appeal, this came out of the £2,029 raised on the Ben Nevis climb.

Then on 22 July 1984 she took part in the Inverness Fun Run and completed the 6¾ miles in 79 minutes, 33 seconds, leaving younger participants in her wake.

From that event she raised £1000 sponsorship for the Inverness and Nairn Multiple Sclerosis Society and League of Friends at Craig Dunain.

Such has been the demand for copies of "A Discarded Brat" Suzie has saved her old age pension week after week to have this third reprint.

For her age and for her stature she is quite an amazing woman.

Her story is a fascinating insight into growing up after being discarded.

It's a sad yet heartening story of achievement against all odds. It's a story I never tire of reading.

W.M. Wilson
Editor in Chief
Highland News Group of Newspapers

A DISCARDED BRAT

ELIZABETH McKAY

First Printing 1980
Second Printing 1981
Third Printing 1985
Fourth Printing 1986
Fifth Printing 1987
Sixth Printing 1989

Printed by
Highland Printers
Henderson Road
Inverness

Preface

Dear Reader,

In writing my autobiography, I felt as if I were speaking to someone and unburdening myself to a friend. It has, somehow, given me great relief and I have not been so lonely — I say this from the bottom of my heart.

There are a number of lonely people in this world who have, like me, passed through many tribulations, sufferings of the body and mind, disappointments and disillusionments. What I have written of, the places, people and incidents, is all based upon true facts.

Ushered into the light of the world unwanted, tossed about in a tumultuous ocean since my cradle days, I was a lonely wanderer drifting wherever the forces of events would carry me, but, with only one object in mind, a yearning to solve the problem of my parentage. Believe me I have not found it easy to fashion out the pattern of my life.

I have spoken of the Highland folk with warmth, and portrayed them in their heritage of vast and rugged grandeur, where their roots lie deep in the heathery glens, picturesque in their Winter slumber. In Springtime when all things grow, and in the efflorescence of Summer and the mellow gold of the Autumn. In the East the dawn and in the West the afterglow of sundown. Vistas of indescribable beauty.

Such is the heart of the Highlands.

The picture I cannot help having in my mind for my book is myself, a little lassie about four-and-a-half years of age, in South Esk Street, Montrose, clad in a tattered skirt and bare-footed with a shawl wrapped round my shoulders, my auburn hair in straggly pigtails. I am sitting huddled against a lamp-post eating a crust of bread which I had greedily snatched out of the gutter. Like the beggar of Scripture I ate the crumbs that fell from the rich man's table. All my life I have been nothing. Thus it was with me.

I am dedicating "A Discarded Brat" to the towns I have been associated with — Edinburgh, Montrose, Inverness and Aberdeen and to Farr, Strathnairn where I spent the seven happiest, most carefree years of my life.

Elizabeth McKay

Philip Demeo — Suzie's father. Gamekeeper to the Duke of Buccleuch at the turn of the century

Foreword

WE ARE all under an obligation to Almighty God to help those poorer and weaker than ourselves regardless of colour or creed. We must never postpone the action we can take to fulfil our obligations. We should not allow personal feelings or opinions stand in our path in bringing a breath of love and justice to those cut off from society who suffer untold distress and desolation. This is the basic foundation of Christian society.

"A Discarded Brat"
Elizabeth McKay, nicknamed Suzie

Elena Demeo — Suzie's sister

Introduction

MY STORY actually begins twelve days before my birth, when a startling and appalling tragedy took place at Tollcross, one of the busiest thoroughfares of Edinburgh.

"THE MURDERED BOY"

as reported in the "SCOTSMAN" of 23rd MARCH, 1909

"Last night, just before darkness set in, the victim being an unoffending boy, six years of age, and the assailant being a powerful Irishman, to whom he was a total stranger. The circumstances of the deed suggest that it was that of a madman, or of someone in the delirium of intoxication.

"The boy, Francis Demeo, resided with his parents at 3 Home Street, immediately adjoining Tollcross. About seven o'clock, when, as usual at that hour, there was a large amount of traffic in the vicinity, numerous tramcars passing, and many persons coming and going on foot, the boy was playing in the street.

"When close to the underground lavatory which is situated in the centre of the roadway at Tollcross, a strongly-built man approached and spoke to him. From the conversation and conduct of the man and boy, those who witnessed the tragedy got the impression that the man was the boy's father, and that he was playfully conversing with him.

"Suddenly, however, to the horror of those who were near the spot, the man was seen to raise the child in his arms, go towards the lavatory and dash the boy over the railings and down the lavatory stair. Immediately several persons rushed at the assailant and overpowered him, while others picked up the boy, who, it was at once apparent, had sustained frightful injuries. He was carried with all haste to the Royal Infirmary. There it was found that his injuries to his head gave no hope of his surviving. He was unconscious: and a few minutes after his admission he succumbed to his injuries.

"Meantime, two constables arrived on the scene of the tragedy, and the assailant was taken into custody and conveyed to the City Police Office. The man is said to have been sober. On the way to the Police Station he sang all the time and was apparently suffering from mental derangement.

"When questioned at the Police Station, the prisoner, who was six feet in height and of powerful build, stated that he was a farmer and belonged to Drumore, County Leitrim, and that he came to this counrty only a few days ago. Since his arrival in Edinburgh he had been staying in a lodging house in Grassmarket. He gave his name as John O'Neill and his age as thirty-six years.

"The boy's mother, on being apprised of what had occurred, hurried to the Infirmary, in spite of the infirm state of her health at the time, and was with her son when he died. Her distraction was painful a feature of the tragedy. On the boy's death she was taken away in a state of collapse. She was a Scotswoman, but her husband was an Italian. They had only recently come to the city from a smaller town, a relative of the father being in business in Edinburgh. The boy had been in the house all day attending upon his mother. After tea he went down to the street in order to be in the fresh air for a little: and thereupon met his death in such a startling and unexpected manner.

"Little is known about the assailant. At the lodging house where he had been staying he seemed not to have been very much noticed. The officials could not recall him to their memory. It was stated, however, that he had been seen in the course of the afternoon behaving in a wild and erratic manner, such as suggested that he had lost his mental balance. It was also stated that he attempted in the course of the day to throw himself in front of a tramcar.

"The affair caused a profound sensation in the district when it became known. In view of the busy public character of the scene, where anyone might expect to be secure from an attack of this kind, a feeling of disquiet and alarm was created. Great sympathy was also felt for the parents in their tragic bereavement.

"O'Neill passed the bar of the City Police Court next day on a charge of murder, and was remitted to the Sheriff."

EXTRACT FROM THE "SCOTSMAN" of 10th MAY, 1909

"At the trial of John O'Neill in the High Court of Justiciary in Edinburgh, 10th May 1909, the jury (as directed by Lord Guthrie), returned a verdict that the accused committed the murder, but that he was insane at the time. They therefore acquitted him on the grounds of insanity.

"Lord Guthrie said an order would be made that, in respect of the verdict of the jury, the Court assoilzied the accused SIMPLICITER, but ordered him to be kept in strict custody at the General Prison in Perth until His Majesty's pleasure be known."

EXTRACT FROM THE "SCOTSMAN" of 29th *MARCH,*
1909

THE EDINBURGH MURDER:
FUNERAL OF THE VICTIM

"Widespread interest in the tragedy at Tollcross, where the six-year-old boy, Frances Demeo, lost his life in such remarkable and painful circumstances, has been shown by the residents of Edinburgh.

"The fact was indicated by the crowds who witnessed the funeral proceedings on Saturday afternoon. An hour before the funeral procession was timed to leave the boy's house at 3 Home Street, a number of persons had assembled on the street in front which was also the scene of the murder. By four o'clock there were thousands gathered at Tollcross, and the police had considerable difficulty in keeping the way clear for the passing traffic. Positions overlooking the centre of interest were fully occupied by spectators. Most of the windows round about had their blinds drawn.

"A sudden hush came over the great crowd as the little white coffin was carried out and placed on the hearse, the men in the crowd uncovering their heads.

"The funeral procession passed slowly down Lothian Road, which was also lined with spectators. The route was by Queensferry Street, and across the Dean Bridge to the Burial ground at Comely Bank. A force of police was in attendance, and the general public were excluded from the graveyard. At the grave, the Service was conducted by the Rev R. L. Jaffrey, St John's.

"Numerous wreaths and crosses were placed on the grave. There was also a large cross of marble, subscribed by the general public, and bearing an inscription.

"The youthfulness of the victim, together with the other circumstances, women amongst the crowd were visibly affected."

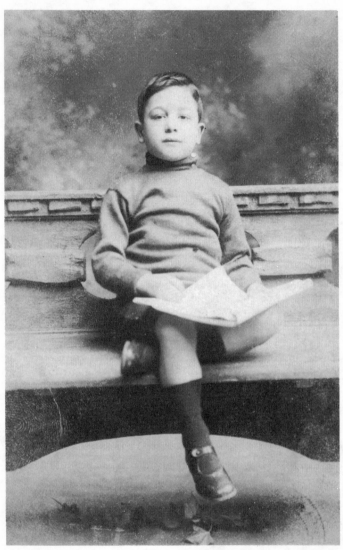

Frances Demeo — Suzie's brother

CHAPTER 1

From a town to a town
To an old world street
Ill-clad and bare-footed
A hungry brat running around

Like gold from the earth
Was a crust from the gutter
To feed the mouth
Of that hungry cratur.

E. McKay

ON THURSDAY, APRIL 3, 1909 at 8.50am at 3 Home Street, Tollcross, Edinburgh, in a three-roomed house, one flight of stairs up, a woman gave birth to a little bundle of humanity. Her mind was almost unhinged with grief at the tragedy already unfolded. Her interest in the young infant had gone, her thoughts all centred entirely on her little dead son, who was six years and nine months old. She was annoyed that her newborn baby had survived the tremendous shock she herself underwent and would not allow the little mite to feed from her breast. Had it not been for the child's Aunt Nellie, the babe might have met the same fate as her brother, Francis, as the mother threatened to do away with her after she was born. As I'm that child, Elizabeth McKay (which is my mother's maiden name, according to my birth lines, I'm entitled to use McKay or Demeo) I can truthfully say there were no happy birthday greetings awaiting me in Auld Reekie, Edinburgh, the capital of Scotland. Only a tragedy over-shadowed the whole atmosphere, casting its reflection on me.

Aunt Nellie, my mother's sister, was almost out of her mind with distraction to know what to do with me, until she remembered an old couple who lived in a two-roomed house in Montrose. Bundling me up, she journeyed down and left me in their care. I do not know what arrangements she made with them, but there I stayed. Their name was Mr and Mrs Farmer, 27 South Esk Street, Montrose.

I have few recollections of those early days. The couple were old, too old to be looking after a child, but they did their utmost.

The old man was a drunkard, and his poor old wife had a struggle to make both ends meet. Any extra money given to her by a friend, she would hide in her little red purse, which she slipped inside the leg of the stocking she was wearing. Often, when the old man was short of cash, he pestered her for some and squandered it on drink. Many a day the poor thing would be breaking her heart weeping. The hardships and toils of life made her old beyond her years. Her health was failing, and she was almost incapable of looking after me. Thus, when I grew older, I was left more or less on my own to roam the streets and alleys, ragged, bare-footed and hungry. So hungry that I was glad to snatch a crust out of the gutter, and wipe the dubs off with my scanty clothing. Sometimes a passer-by would give me a handful of boiled winkles to eat using a pin to pick the slug out of its shell, which I relished, At times a neighbour would take pity on me, offer me a piece of bread and a bowl of soup, which I supped greedily. My playground was more or less round about the harbour, where I loved to sit and dangle my legs over the jetty. Time and again I would be sent home by the quayside workers for fear I would fall in. Often I would wander into the fish shed and watch the fish wives gut and salt the herrings. Before dusk came down, I trailed after Leerie, the lamp-lighter. I could scarcely keep pace with him as he strode along from lamp-post to lamp-post with his gas wand, which was a long pole, and with a pilot light at the end, he lit up the gas mantles — not forgetting the very narrow closes with their gas lamps hanging from wall brackets, thus giving the atmosphere an old world and stage effect. When tired I scooted off home to roost with the old man and the old woman. Scrambling over the top of them to the back of the bed I huddled down beneath the unkempt bed clothes with my dummy teat, my sole companion and comforter.

On one occasion I tramped on a broken beer bottle and a piece was stuck in the sole of my foot. I remembered it so well, as if it were yesterday as I crippled indoors weeping, crying out "my foot, my foot, bad bottle". The old man laid me on the living-room table, and extracted the piece of beer bottle. The wound, not being properly cleaned, festered, and if one of the neighbours had not applied a porridge poultice, goodness only knows what might have happened. Once during that period while sitting on the edge of the pavement, two dogs came sniffing around me, and started barking. I fear they had scented the porridge. I screamed and tried to cover my foot with my tattered skirt until some passer-by came to my rescue. There were happier times too, when the old man dressed me up and took me round the shops, and with an odd copper we bought some pies. The paper bag clutched in my hand, I tugged him along the street, for I couldn't get home quick enough to deposit the bag in the old women's lap, who would be patiently sitting by the fireside awaiting our return. Having a great fondness for horses, I recall once, when one was standing by the kerb outside the door, I put my two hands round one of his fetlocks and did my utmost to lift up his hoof. The horse seemed to sense what I was about so he gracefully lifted it up for me, after my careful examination he quickly put it down. To me horses are the noblest of all animals.

I started school at five years of age. Often I was bothered with nose bleedings and the teacher would lay me flat on my back on the floor. I have a faint recollection her name was Miss Brown. I recall taking the whooping cough and so stayed away from school.

The "Whipper In" (Janitor), as he was usually called, saw me on the street one day and lifted me up in his arms, with the intention of taking me to school, but my cries brought the old man shuffling out to the door. He dared the "Whipper

In" to lay his hands on me, so he slunk off like a dog with its tail between its legs after being scolded.

My dummy teat I took to school and now and again had a go at it. One day the old woman was sitting by the fire, all dressed up ready to go to hospital, she was crying like to break her heart. She was only gone a week when her remains came home. Her coffin was placed on top of the bed in the little back room. I remember the old man lifted me up and carried me through to see her. She looked so still, and oh, so cold! I felt scared, and hid my face in the old man's neck, crying out, "Give her some tea". The day of the funeral, the coffin had to go out of the front room window on to the pavement owing to the nasty bend in the doorway. In the little back room, on the chesterfield, stood a large glass oval-shaped case. Inside all kinds of artificial fruits and leaves, many a time I climbed on to a chair and gripping the edge with my fingers, drew myself up on my toes, gazed at it for long enough, almost mesmerised.

My guardian seemed lost, there was just the two of us now. He did his best to keep me clean, and I can still see him sitting on a chair near the window, his great big hands trying to comb my hair and get me ready for school, also prepare a kind of a meal. Then, alas, a week later, coming home from school, I found the door jammed. I struggled with the knob and kicked the panel. Someone came to my aid and forced the door open. To my horror the old man was lying behind the door, as if dead. He was helped up and word sent to the doctor. I looked up into the old man's face. He was so very tall — I imagine he would be six feet in height. I can still hear the doctor in a most abrupt manner say, "Speak, man speak". The old man couldn't speak. Shortly after I saw him stretched out on a long board, supported by two chairs near the bedside. My whole world had suddenly become empty. I felt lost and bewildered, alone in the room it had a most alarming effect on me, with no one to speak to and no one to run to, and the house in semi-darkness as the late after-

4

noon was drawing to a close I stood and looked at the old man who no longer could speak to me, stricken with fear and engulfed in loneliness and desolation which I could not disentangle. I crept out and sat on the door step huddled up resting my head on my knees, and fell asleep, later to be rudely awakened and hustled off to the workhouse. The street lamps were aglow, for Leerie the lamplighter had been and gone.

CHAPTER 2

THIS WAS my first glimpse of a Work House. I found comfort in sitting with the old folk, but sad to say, every time I went into the dining-hall for my meals, along with the inmates, the Matron had a habit of giving me a shove on the back, which made me so miserable. One day I was tracing my finger over the window pane, so the starchy-faced Matron took the opportunity and gave me a whipping. I sobbed and shied away from her, I had never before felt the weight of any human hand on my body. The old man and the old woman, poverty stricken as they were, and in spite of his weakness for a drink, never once raised a hand to strike me, or would allow anyone else to do so, no matter how tiresome I would be. Their patience was beyond measure.

In the Work House, if I remember right, the spacious living room was upstairs and the dining-hall just across from it and the ward, where I slept, was quite near. Usually, I was bedded very early. I recall one night when lying in bed listening to the melodious voices of the fish-wives with their creels roped on their backs, crying out "Fresh herring, fresh herring", mingled with the cries of the fishermen, strutting up and down with their barrows, laden with all kinds of shellfish. It was like music to my ears, and lulled me to sleep. Sometime after midnight I woke up shouting, "Fresh herring, fresh herring. Who'll buy my fresh herring". I put my foot in it, for the whole ward was in an uproar, all over the head's of fresh herrings in the early hours of the morning. The old people were given no handkerchiefs so they had to use news-papers, which they cut into squares. After use they threw them into the coal fire, copying them, I did likewise.

As for the old men, they had their own quarters. I used to watch them potter in the back garden smoking short clay pipes, some of them would chew their tobacco and then spit it out.

One day a man and a woman arrived in a car to escort me back to Edinburgh to my mother, but apparently she would have nothing to do with me, so I was dumped on to an Aunt Annie Forbes, a half-sister of my mother's who lived at No. 2 Hawthornbank Buildings, Dean Village.

The Matron of the workhouse has long since passed on.

CHAPTER 3

At almost six years old I went to live with my Aunt Annie in a two-roomed house, perched on the summit of a lofty bank overlooking the River Dean, whose gulfy torrents poured down like waterfalls, winding its way through the heart of the Dean Village, with the old-fashioned quaint shaped houses, and red tiled roofs with their crow-stepped gables and the old clock tower in its unique setting and in the distance the mighty Dean Bridge, spanning the river bearing the weight of the traffic to and fro. A picturesque view presented itself to me where ever I turned my eyes.

Aunt Annie who was a widow, had to go out daily and work for her livelihood. She had one of a family, a laddie called Jack, very much pampered by his mother. My cousin and I attended the Dean Village school and the little Mission Hall of St Mary's Episcopal Church on the cobbled brae. For a while I thought I was in a new world. A gentleman visited me regularly every weekend and stayed till Monday. He taught me to call him Papa, and I looked forward so eagerly to his visits. He was always so kind and gentle. I usually slept with my Aunt, but when my Papa came, I had to sleep with him. Before retiring to bed, he taught me to go down on my knees and make the Sign of the Cross, clasping my hands together and say my Prayers. Alas, one weekend he did not come. I felt lost and afraid, something like a pang entered my heart that I should never see him again. I wept and longed for the protection and comfort of his arms. Every day I looked up and down the streets and byways, listening for the sound of his footsteps coming down the cobbled brae. But all in vain. I never saw my Papa again. In appearance he was a tall, well-built man, and always he donned a long black cloak with a cape attached. Cloaks were seemingly the fashion in those days.

> *Dear Papa, dear Papa, come back and see me,*
> *Sit me again upon your knee*
> *And sing to me the song of the Deep,*
> *That cradled me and hushed me down to sleep,*
> *Dear Papa, dear Papa, come back to me.*
>
> *E. McKay*

After this catastrophe my whole world suddenly came to an end. I was no longer the carefree, happy child and I felt myself neglected. My Aunt's attitude towards me was entirely changed. No longer had she the same interest in my welfare. Aunt Annie was a tall, handsome woman, and exceptionally good-looking and always the centre of attraction. She loved company, especially uniforms. The War being on, Edinburgh was full of troops drafted from all parts of the globe. Where ever you went you heard a War-time ditty being sung in the streets. I just remember two of them. "Keep the Home Fires Burning" and "Don't forget your Soldier Laddie".

7

Aunt not only loved companionship, but also was very fond of a wee dram, and so was never without a bottle of something or other. She had a most charming manner and could twist the opposite sex round her little finger. It was a case of "Come into my parlour said the spider to the fly". Young as I was, my eyes witnessed many queer goings-on, all very strange and foreign to me. I was still very much troubled with nose bleedings when bending over my books. I remember once, during playtime on the swings, one of the older children pushed me far too high, with the result that I lost my grip and was thrown and came down with such force on the concrete giving my forehead a sickening thud. The teacher very kindly sent me home. Little sympathy was shown either by my cousin or his mother.

My Aunt Annie gradually became a heavy drinker and there wasn't a night of the week but she was out with her friends, and I was shown the outside of the door. How I dreaded being left out so long, crouched down by the side of the River Dean, clinging to the railings, my cries of heartbreak drowned by the roaring waters, until a neighbour, taking a last look round before retiring to bed, noticing my pitiful plight piloted me into her home and sat me down comfortably by the fireside and a glass of hot milk. I remained there until the early hours of next morning when Auntie and her associates would come tottering down the cobbled brae hanging on to each other, all being the worse of drink. They were singing at the pitch of their voices. What a hullabaloo they made. Auntie would come staggering up to one of the neighbouring windows giving it a none too canny rap, doing her best to make herself sound polite, and cry in a high-pitched parrot-like voice, "Is wee Lizzie in?" You can imagine what it sounded like under the influence of drink, so I, "the brat", as I was often called, would jump up my eyes on my rescuer, filled with a mixture of tears and gratitude for a few hours spent in homely comfort, before making my reluctant retiral. On entering the house, I usually received a box on the ear, and was shoved through to the other room out of the way. My cousin, a tall, hefty lad, and a few years my elder, had little difficulty in getting in to the house if the door was locked, he simply heaved himself on to the sill, hauled down the window and clambered in over the top. No bother at all! I remember once my cousin taking me to the cinema. To my eyes it was just a mass jumble of silent movie pictures which I did not understand.

Early one evening Aunt Annie was preparing to go out when a well-dressed woman called to see her. I felt she had come to take Auntie away for the evening and I was terrified that I would be left out again on the banks of the Dean for yet another night. Not always did a kindly neighbour come to my rescue. This evening I broke down and clung to my Auntie's skirt, pleading with her to take me along with her. The other woman, on hearing my cries, let out with her foot and kicked me. Taken off my guard I stumbled and fell. For the moment I felt stunned, then I picked myself up, gazing from one to the other, especially at the strange woman, as much as to say, "What did *you* do that for?" In the end I was taken with them to spend the evening in some house where a number of my Aunt's associates were gathered. I can remember being bustled along with four or five children belonging to the house into an untidy looking bed in the corner of the room to play, so as to be out of the way while my Aunt and her friends lounged round the living room. Most of them were soldiers. The woman of the house sat by the fireside with her youngest on her knee, feeding it at the bare breast, now and again, she would squirt her milk over her guests. There would be a shuffling of chairs and roars of laughter.

The evening passed with the popping of corks and then a sing-song. Time went by unchecked. They were all as drunk as could be. Then an argument arose. Zero hour was at hand. Suddenly bottles and glasses went whizzing like rockets through the air. Dishes were broken and one of the soldiers was badly cut on the side of the face. The blood was pouring and the others were more or less scratched and bruised. The bairns and I in the bed started a howling match. Owing to the din, our cries were drowned while our superiors were steeped in drunkenness and squabble. How my Aunt and I got home that night I have no recollection.

CHAPTER 4

Nine months passed, and Aunt Annie began to show more than ever that I was unwanted, so one day she dressed me up with special care and took me a short journey. We arrived at a large building where we were ushered into a hall. A woman appeared in a white uniform. I stood clutching my Aunt's skirt tightly while they exchanged words. Then Auntie began disengaging my hands from her clothes and showed signs of going. I suddenly realised that she was leaving me behind and started crying, "Don't go away, don't leave me — please!" and clutched her skirt all the more tightly. In the end the woman had to drag me away, while I screamed and struggled to run after my Aunt as I watched her disappearing from my sight. I was taken into a room just off the front hall, and seated on a mat in front of the fire, surrounded by a number of toys but still sobbing and bewildered at the sudden turn of things, my equilibrium was completely upset. A short while ago I was in my Aunt's house in the Dean Village now I was back in the Workhouse, this time Craiglockhart Workhouse. I remember the room they put me in, turned out to be a ward with two rows of beds occupied by inmates, spotlessly clean. After I had quietened down, the nurse undressed me and plumped me into the bath which stood in the corner of the ward. Tears were soon forgotten as I splashed in the soapy water. The Doctor came in and the nurse stood me on the table, clothed only in Nature's attire, and as he looked at me he remarked to the nurse, "What a wee bairn". My stay at the Workhouse was short, and I was admitted to Balgreen Orphanage out the Gorgie Road, belonging to the Edinburgh Parish Council, whose offices are in Castle Terrace. The Orphanage was a fine old rambling house, surrounded by spacious grounds, lawns and walks, bordered with flower beds, shrubs and trees.

> *"Trees that look at God all day*
> *And lift their leafy arms to pray . . ."*

The children had plenty of scope and freedom, romping about the most beautifully kept lawns. At the back of the building were swings, see-saws and other such like out-door amusements. They were loved and well-cared for, clothed and well-fed. During the short spell at the Orphanage, it was quite a change to be among a different class of people. At first I felt strange and fluttered around like a frightened bird. Seeing all things were well I gradually came out of my shell. I cannot remember much about the school I attended, only that in the mornings we were formed into two groups, Protestants and Catholics, I lined up with the Protestants. I have a faint recollection of going into the school dining-room where we were served with hot dinners. There was no scarcity of food, and we had more than ample. Every Saturday we had our heads looked over and small tooth-combed with carbolic lotion. The smell was quite pleasant. I mixed with the children and took part in the indoor and outdoor amusements. Sometimes a few of them were inclined to torment me, saying I had a face like a monkey. I got into the habit of shading my face with my hand whenever anyone spoke to me. Folk put it down to shyness, but little did they know. (The monkey who sees, hears and speaks no evil, whose intelligence is more than ants and less than human beings). I recall once in the early hours of the morning being awakened from slumber and having to come downstairs where campbeds were set up owing to the War, Auld Reekie was receiving a taste of Jerry's bombs, whistling through the air like fire rockets, illuminating the sky till it was like a blazing sea of fire. Oft times I would potter off on my own through the grounds, my eyes viewing the work of Nature's artistry with admiration, but for all that, my thoughts would still wander back to Montrose, to an old man and an old woman whose passing away I had witnessed.

CHAPTER 5

Hail to the capital of the Highlands,
Inverness, where proudly she stands
Surrounded by her kilted clans
Regardless of domination

Far down in history on Culloden Moor
A bloody battle raged
To fix the price on Cumberland's head
And win the Crown for Charlie.

From over the hills and far beyond
Stole the hearts of the loyal Scots,
And to the skirl of the pipes they rallied around
To behold their Prince on Highland ground.

Surrounded by heather, myrtle and peat,
Which for many a day was to keep warm his feet,
And cradle his fair head down to sleep,
Our Royal Prince from over the Deep.

E. McKay

SOMETIME IN the year 1916 from Balgreen Orphanage, I was boarded out, at seven years of age, by the Edinburgh

Parish Council, to nine miles west of the Capital of the Highlands, Inverness, Eastern Cottage, Farr, Strathnairn, is a semi-detached two-story house, situated by the main roadside on Farr Estate, built by the estate workers in the year 1907. This you will see inscribed on the wall at the east side. The house has a lovely wide verandah, supported by red painted wooden pillars in their natural state, entwined by a climbing rose tree, one of the deep red ones, and a flower garden in front, and at the back a large piece of ground with out-houses, any amount of berry bushes of all kinds, a few silver birches, boxes of bees and hives, also some hens. On the opposite side of the road is the forest, at the gable end of the house over the fence in the park stands an old flowering cherry tree, and in the month of May is a picture for the eye to behold. The park is kept more or less for sheep, especially at lambing time. The west side is bound by a burn which runs underneath the main road. In the distance are patches of woods, warrens covered with bracken, and far beyond, the dark moorland with its deep peat bogs sweeping higher and higher, and lochs and rivers and ranges of hills, their heather clad slopes dotted with little thatched cottages, and a shooting box here and there. I can recall lonely keeps and ruined homesteads sheep tracks and silent glens, mingling with the scent of the wild bog myrtle.

Miss Barbara Fraser with whom I stayed was born in a house a little way west of the road called Sockich which her grandfather built, with a small croft attached. When her father died, to make room for the next generation, Miss Fraser and her aged mother moved to a small cottage within sight of Farr Lodge gates. Soon after this her mother passed on. The cottage, being so very old, it was beginning to crumble so the old Laird, Mr MacKenzie of Farr, gave orders for it to be demolished, and a new one built in its place. While "Eastern and Western Cottages" were being built, Auntie Barbara stayed in the old schoolhouse at "Dalvourn".

Auntie Barbara, as I was brought up to call her, was a

wonderful old lady of sixty-seven years of age, who went out of her way to give me a real home. At first I caused considerable excitement among the neighbouring folk. News travels fast on the News Reel, but it travelled a lot faster in a country community. The postman on his daily rounds would be stopped by some of the local folk. The topic of the conversation would be the newcomer to the Strath. "Have you heard the latest news? Old Barbara has got a little lassie, and she has come all the way from Edinburgh". Soon I was well acquainted with all. Such hospitality they had to give, poor as some of them were, I was made more than welcome to share. They had a kind look for everyone striving along the daily road, who in return, would pass it on and help to lift another's load.

In those days a pony trap from Aberarder was the only conveyance to Inverness, driven by one of the local folk. It could only accommodate two or three passengers, also collected the mail and delivered it to Farr Post Office, not forgetting newspapers such as the "Courier" and the "Northern Chronicle".

I made friends with old Mrs MacKenzie of Farr, who was extremely kind to me. When out walking with her two big labradors, she would never pass without calling. If you didn't happen to see her coming in the garden gate, you heard the lilt of her voice calling, "Are you in Barbara?", and oh dear! when the dogs bounded in, the living room was in uproar. The panicky cats would go scurrying in all directions, I remember a remark Mrs MacKenzie made about my teeth, that they were good, and I must look after them and keep them clean. Auntie assured her that it was quite a job making me clean them without incurring a howling match. Little wonder when I had to use salt or soot. On their return trip from Henley-on-Thames, Mr and Mrs MacKenzie never forgot to bring a gift to each and all their tenants. I remember the last gift I, myself received. It was a red book called "Faithful Soldiers". They were well respected and loved by all

14

who knew them, and mingled freely with the tenants, spoke their language, shared their feelings and treated them with sympathy and kindness. Mrs MacKenzie would take me round the garden and teach me the names of the flowers and trees. One special tree she dearly loved was the May tree, I recall her saying she was christened after it. O ne such tree grew inside Farr Lodge gates beside the avenue and in summer, was a mass of pink blossom. There wasn't a house on their estate that didn't display a photograph of Mr and Mrs MacKenzie of Farr on their mantlepiece. Mrs MacKenzie of Farr in all appearances resembled Queen Alexandra.

CHAPTER 6

FARR PUBLIC SCHOOL, which I attended lay about two miles east the road, as there was no conveyance, I naturally had a good walk ahead of me. Sometimes I was fortunate in being offered a lift in a passing vehicle or a pony and trap, but there was nothing I liked better than sitting up beside the driver of a long lorry loaded with tree trunks on its way to Daviot Station. Most mornings, on my arrival at school after my long walk, I felt more inclined to sleep than settling down to studies. Often I seemed to drift away somewhere on the edge of life's sea, when suddenly I would feel the sharp probe of the master's pointer, or my ear being pulled, jerking me out of a dreamy abstraction, into which I had sunk. His voice grated with a slight touch of annoyance as he remarked, "Come along, dreamer, wake up". My intellect being dull, I could not grasp the full knowledge put before me, and it worried me unduly. Thus I was forced to fall back in class, amidst the titterings of my mates wishing with all my heart I could silence those spiteful creatures. It preyed so much on my mind that when the shrill blast, like a policeman's whistle called us at playtime, I dreaded having to file into that depressing atmosphere of drab tasks that lay within the walls of the school of learning. Always my eyes travelled to my name on the large blackboard, where a long winding trail of errors, from yesterday's dictation, etc, awaited me. Often the pupils sitting nearest would provoke me, taking advantage when the masters' back was turned, and whisper in my ear, "Hey Liz! Have you looked at the blackboard?" With a grin like a Cheshire cat on my face, I unwillingly nodded, feeling irritable, which was as far as I got, when the master would swiftly turn with his piercing eye fixed upon us, from beneath beetling eyebrows that would cause the boldest to quail before him. Silence would reign over the class, all very studious with faces like saints, but when playtime came the devil of saints were we. Boys and girls mingling, taking part in all the school games, putting the stone, tossing the caber, high jump, long jump, racing and tug-of-war, not forgetting outrageous fights, which were part and parcel of school days. We girls received the worst end of the stick, our hair almost pulled out by the roots, the crack of a shinty club across our legs, we pelted one another with clods or anything that came within reach of our hands. Amidst shouts and shrieks echoing through the Strath, as if the gathering of the clans had come together again to meet in deadly combat. Those of us who watched, whooped and jumped egging on the fight. Our clothes, being a good length, would be a bit of a nuisance at times getting in the way, especially when climbing trees, turning the cattie or scrambling over dykes, fences and gates, or playing at leapfrog, the boys could see us far enough their heads getting entangled in our fal-de-rals. There was wholehearted joy amongst boys and girls alike. Here we learned to give and take, which is the true spirit of sportsmanship. Football was the most popular game, but I'm afraid it too was more like a bitter fight than an ordinary pastime. Here there was no obvious rules and referees, there was only the one rule to get the ball into the opponent's goal by any means short of murder. The only qualifications were strength, enthusiasm and a complete indifference to mud and dripping clothes.

16

On arriving home after some of those bitter fights, I would approach the house stealthily, tip-toe in and creep upstairs to my bedroom, to try and make myself a little presentable for, indeed, I was in a frightful mess, dishevelled from head to foot, but it was always the same, caught in the act, half-way up, I blamed the cats for giving the show away, as they seemed to be forever on the prowl and nothing ever escaped them. They insisted on purring and fussing round my legs and now and again they would let out a mew. It was hopeless making a sign to them to shut up, for they simply ignored it and, of course, Auntie Barbara having very sharp ears would come and investigate, and almost took a fit when she saw me. "Mercy me, what in the world have you been up to now? Just look at your clothes, you limmer". Silent and hang-dog, shuffling from foot to foot, mumbling something or other, "I'm sorry", looking and fingering my clothes. I can still hear her saying, "Your sorrow becomes you. If you had to wash and mend them, you would take better care of your clothes". My hair, in which Auntie took such pride, hung down my back like rats tails, as she, herself, termed it, and my face as black as the crook, my pinafore torn, my stockings hanging like a concertina, as I had lost my garters. Now and again I would give them a hitch up, but oh me the day, I wish you had seen Auntie Barbara, she was like a hen on a hot girdle. In those days the fashion in clothes was slightly different from what they wear today. Some of the boys wore high stiff collars, tight fitting double seated knicker-bockers buttoned below the kneecap, and hand-knitted hose, and sprigged boots with iron toe bits, I must confess, I was all clothes together. The old folk believed in having plenty on, for fear of catching your death of cold.

CHAPTER 7

SOMETIMES DURING lessons we would snap our fingers and ask the Master "to leave the room". In those days the term used for toilet was "Privy" which was a wee shed at the foot of the playground with a pail inside a wooden seat resembling a commode and a bunch of newspapers stuck in the corner. There were no wash-hand basins. When school was over the master just emptied the pail over the dyke into the wood — no bother at all! The drinking water was from a tap outside in the wall beside the boys' cloakroom. You had to bend down and put your mouth to it.

On our way home from school if the unlooked-for situation arose, we would make a hasty retreat to a public "convenience" behind a bush by the road-side or into a wood, taking good care there were no nettles or prickly branches before sitting back on our hunkers, using a bit of moss or a docken leaf or anything that came within reach of our hands, to serve the purpose. Nae bother a'va!

Very often when school was over I was compelled to stay behind owing to my lessons not being up to the mark, but I never seemed to get anywhere. Giving way to sobs, my sums and my writing on my slate would be blotched with tears. When allowed to go home the Master's wife would meet me coming out with a piece and jam. As I plodded home wearily I missed the companionship of the scholars going my way and somehow the road seemed longer, especially when the month of October marched in bearing the finger-print of Autumn. The clocks put back an hour, evening shadows would suddenly deepen, and the earth seemed to waken mysteriously playing false tricks on my imagination, queer shapes loomed ominously around me. Bats screeched and swerved at nothing in the air above me. I could hear the continual hooting of that nightly visitor, the owl, the bellowing of the deer on their way down from the hills looking for food, and the eerie cries of the birds, with the scream of a hawk as if pouncing on its prey. The wind was moaning through the woods and the trees were pressing their branches close together whispering and murmuring and sighing. Those sounds to which I had listened so many times lying in bed at night

18

all seemed uncanny and gave me strange, weird feelings as if the whole Strath was haunted. Several times Auntie Barbara came to meet me and found me crouching in the shadows by the roadside hardly daring to breathe, What a relief it was to hear the lilt of her soft Highland accent calling, "Lizzie, are you there?"

Dear Reader,

I almost forgot to mention the strap which was a long narrow piece of leather with three fingers. The Master being a strict disciplinarian made good use of it for not paying attention to our studies and for carelessness and not forgetting our devilment. Oft-times he would place the strap near the coal fire to harden. Those of us about to be punished had to line up on our way out at the eleven o'clock play, the Master holding the strap over his right shoulder ready for action, while we were keyed up to high doh, rubbing and blowing our hands, Everytime I held out mine I recoiled and drew back my hand, eventually the strap caught up and lashed down twice as hard, its long snake-like fingers curling round my wrist leaving its trademark. I have a faint recollection that one of the boys refused to come forward so the Master had no alternative but to take him by the scruff of the neck and drag him through to the small room and give him three of the best on the backside. Sometime after I left school I heard he was reported and that he was reprimanded by the court for being too severe, I understand he was reprimanded a second time.

I recall Auntie Barbara telling me that Mr MacRae's predecessor, a Mr MacBeth, was painted a strict disciplinarian, his pupils secretly got hold of his strap and decided to get rid of it by throwing it up through the ventilator in the roof of the schoolroom; there were a few anxious moments, it was like the impossible so like Bruce and the spider they tried again and again, taking turns they finally succeeded as it disappeared into utter darkness, its charmed life came to an end. That must have been more than seventy years ago.

24th March, 1977. It is interesting to know that after I had related the incident to Mrs Lamont, the head teacher, that at the Farr Public School, Strathnairn Centenary Celebrations 2nd April, 1977 the strap located in the ventilator was on display.

CHAPTER 8

SCHOOL DINNERS were unheard of, so we carried in our schoolbags a lunch, a bottle of milk and a good piece, this was to sustain us throughout the day, until we arrived home from school. The folk here in the Strath had more or less their dinner at night, owing to their men-folk working distances away, they too would carry a piece in their satchel.

Some of the scholars going to school had greater distances to cover, and would have to leave their homes very early in the morning, taking a shortcut across the lonely moors and burns and rivers bridged here and there with narrow foot planks thrown across or a kind of bridge with a length of wire on both sides to hold on to, put up by some of the local folk, which were often swept away by the stormy weather. One person crossing one of those bridges over the River Nairn lost his life. On most wintery days the scholars would take to the rough hill tracks, known as roads, where country carts pitched and jostled over deep ruts and stones like wagons in the Wild West. They would pursue their journey struggling against stormy winds and blizzards, snowflakes whirling with fury. Those hardy wee Highlanders liked nothing better than to battle against the elements. But, there were days when one could not wade through the snowdrifts, or buffet the successive snow-storms which swept down with blinding fury from the hills. In the melancholy twilight stars like infinite small jewels twinkled in the clear sky, the moon rising palely through

Whispering Winds

My progress was slow through the struggling years
but now there's a song in my heart
as I relive my childhood days
a discarded brat in a lovely Highland Strath.

Nature's astir Spring in the air as I take to the
Highway nine miles west of my adopted Inverness
The Capital of the Highlands where proudly it stands
speaks and breathes of bygone glory where once the
country's heros mustered in strength their kilts and
plaids swinging to the skirl of the pipes, the glitter of
steel and clang of sword on shield forever echoes
across the great rolling hills.
Now I'm back on the humpty backet road, the rustling breath
of the whispering winds serenading me on and on like
loves old sweet song back home to where I belong
nearer and nearer to the sweet scents of past yesterdays
In a lovely Highland Strath.

Oh Strathnairn bonnie Strathnairn cradled in a
paradise of vast and rugged grandeur here the trees
shimmered and sparkled as the wee birdies sang their
love song to the morn, all seemed to wave a welcome to
me in this heaven on earth.

How my aching heart cries out as I dream of the
mystic folk I used to know who spoke with a gentle old
world courtesy where their roots grew deep in the heathery
glens and where I no longer was one in a crowd and one
all alone, and no longer a victim of despair; for oh the
warmth of their welcome aye brought tears to my eyes when
one of a circle by their firesides, there would be fun and
laughter, fireside stories and legends galore, at the sound
of music from an old melodeon singing and dancing began
till eleven o'clock chimed then good nights, a hearty shake
of the hand and haste ye back again.

Recalling to mind when we were bairnies small chasing
here and there, racing across the windswept moors
and feel the rain like needles on our cheeks
roamed in the haunts of the deer by loch and stream, and
Oh to watch the sunset cast its spell and slowly go down on
Bonnie Strathnairn.

But Oh to wander by my own wee house and dream of my
childhood there, and view the flowering cherry tree that's aye
so dear to me where my heart will ever be in a
Lovely Highland Strath.

by 'a discarded brat'
Elizabeth McKay (Suzie) 9 May 1984

Achnacarry Castle

© Lochiel, K.T.

the trees, and the warm amber lights of the farm houses, crofts and cottages not forgetting the wee but-an-ben reflecting on the snow-white scene, looking misty and ghostly, At this time when everywhere the days are short, and so much shut in by hills, it is shorter still, and in those stormy days it is shortest of all. One dresses by candlelight and breakfasts in half-day light, while what is called daylight is rapidly retreating by the late afternoon. There with the blinds drawn, a log and peat fire in the hearth, and the oil lamps glowing, newspapers, books and someone dropping in for a ceilidh, while outside the wind bellowed, whirling snowflakes beat on the pane, and the fierce blast of the storm crashing and howling, we were snug within those sturdy walls. Many a time I woke during the night to the rendering crack of wind thrown trees near the house. The wind was shrieking, scattering buckets, and garden tools noisily at the back of the house, which made sleep difficult. I tried to rest with the bedclothes over my ears. That morning there were trees down everywhere. It was no easy task, when east and west met with all hands on deck, shovels, horses harnessed to snow-ploughs working feverishly clearing the deep wreaths from roads and tracks, where the storm had blown with fierce and bitter blast into the most romantic grotesque shapes. Such is a winter in the Highlands.

When Nature was in one of her various moods the mail from Inverness would be carried on horseback ridden by the son of Mr Goodall, proprietor of Flichity Hotel. On one occasion such was the state of the weather that his father had to take out his horse-drawn carriage with runners and oh! the excitement of us scholars when offered a lift on our way to school, the horses straining to avoid deep snow drifts and the thrill of listening to the sledge-bells jingling across the snow.

The folk in the Strath were very good at foreseeing the weather beforehand and would make preparations to provide a good stock of the essentials such as oatmeal, flour and salt herrings, etc, to tide them over the stormy weather.

CHAPTER 9

TODAY NATURE is astir, the supreme blender of colour, as my thoughts wander back to my childhood days in the heart of the Highlands. It takes but a trivial thing — a scent, a colour, a sound — to remind me and I hug them close fearing that some detail might escape. The sun striking across the wooded slopes, carpeted with primroses, wood anemones and blue-bells, pushing their way out to spread their gospel. Here the great trees shimmered and sparkled in their virgin green. Their beauty and wonder are beyond man's power to describe. The birds trilling like Prima Donnas, beaks brimming with news, for it was the wooing season. I recall Auntie Barbara saying she could hear familiar words in their song, "Oh, Strathnairn, Bonnie Strathnairn". I, too, would lend an ear and listen to their warbling notes.

I still hid my face with my hand when ever anyone spoke to me. Eventually, I grew out of the habit but, every time I met some of the local folk, including Mr MacKenzie, the shepherd, with his long, flowing white beard, they would tease me saying, "Liz, hide your face, hide your face".

Gradually the lambing time began. In the mornings I woke to the sound of lambs' voices as they followed the ewes across the closely bitten turf. On Farr Estate the sheep have a wide range of natural grazing. Every year I accompanied Mr MacKenzie, the shepherd, across the soft grass to see the beginning of life. The flock dotted here and there within a bay of emerald green, gently cropping the grass. One day we came upon two newborn lambs, still warm and wet. They appeared to be all leg and heads. Mr MacKenzie bent down and took hold of one and cleaned its mouth, then thrust his fingers between its jaws. Suddenly there was a shudder, the choking intake of breath, a quiver ran through its gawky little body, its flanks began to swell, then relaxed and then, lo and behold, out into the morning air came the first distinctive "baa!" All this time its mother waited nervously near by, but as soon as we moved away, she bounded forward with an answering call and with an ever ready lick of the tougue. Shortly after they were both up on their legs drawing their first milk. Many a time I've helped the shepherd to extricate a lamb caught bv its fleece in the undergrowth, then giving a "baa" she would slip off to her mother. I recall the joy it gave me when he put a young lamb into my arms to fondle. On one occasion he repeated to me, "A red sky in the morning is the shepherd's warning, a red sky at night is the shepherd's delight".

CHAPTER 10

MEMORIES OF youth are always the most vivid, as I see again my old home. The Spring of the year is just passing into early Summer. The dew of a May morning is supposed to bestow the gift of beauty of those who wash their faces in it. Child-like, I believed it, just as I did in Santa Claus, so sure enough, at the break of dawn, I would rise and join the winged messengers to welcome a new born day. Making a dive for the old flowering cherry tree, her mantle full of blossom, hanging heavily like melting snow, climbing up in to her leafy arms, I gently shook her, bringing down a shower of sparkling dew-drops that drenched me, my hair decked here and there with falling petals. From amidst a garland of dew-wet blossoms, listening to the birds singing their unknown chorus I felt that no human voice could equal the satisfaction it brought to my ears.

Weather permitting I went bare-footed for now I could run with the swiftness and freedom of Nature. Like the rest of the children I followed suit, with or without permission, I would travel about half-a-mile and dispose of my boots and stockings and hide them in a hole in the dyke till I came out of school when I deemed it prudent to put them on again, first of all taking good care to wash my feet in some burn. Some of the boys wore kilts and sporrans and didn't half make them wiggle-waggle showing off their sturdy legs and bare-feet, a fascinating picture of young Highlanders. I remember Auntie Barbara once saying, "Ne'er change a cloot, till May be oot".

In Summer I loved to roam the countryside with its agriculture and horticultural boundaries, a profusion of whin and broom, which looked like a carpet of gold, the scent of hay ever in the air, young corn tossing in silver waves and the joy it gave me listening to the cries of the Golden Plover and Peewits, circling high above the sunny landscape, the silvery notes of the lark. Butterflies danced airily from flower to flower and the bees droned upon the blossoms, lambs frolicked, young foals frisked in the pasture, black and white, and red and brown heifers and calves grazed peacefully blowing their sweet breath through their nostrils into the air already sweet with Hawthorn blossom. Near at hand sounded the piping of the Yellow Hammer, Farr Highland ponies stood under the shade of the great trees, their heads resting on each other's necks, and often they would take spells of washing each other's backs, a case of "You wash my back and I'll wash yours". In the shadowed pasture, young rabbits hopped cautiously out of their burrow: at the least sound of my feet they would scamper for the undergrowth, stupidly pausing, just before they disappeared into their burrow, making a target for a moment's noisy sport; nearby the faint rustling in the long grass, from roving field mice, which often found their way in to the house.

It was sunny and warm with blue skies as I made my way taking a path alongside the fields, I waded breast-high through a heaving gentle sea of wild flowering growth till I came to the River Fearorach, a tributary of the River Nairn, Tracks and water take their own sweeps and bends like musical notes almost touching each other. In the background the low lying hills of Creag na Gobhair. Here I paddled in the river and watched the brown trout like shadows dart to and fro, I scrambled up the bank to where birds nests are so cunningly hidden, and oh! the thrill it gave me when I found a Jenny Wren's quaint wee housie. I recall evenings when the escaping sun set all on fire with its flaming rays, as it slipped below the horizon. This scene was rendered more beautiful, as I listened with rapture to the lowing of the cattle seen coming home in the gloaming and making for their respective quarters of ancient beams and bracken scented stalls, with almost the intelligence of human beings. I sat down and pressed myself against the warm bosom of Mother Earth. The call of the hills, moors and rivers and, oh! the call of the curlew singing its wild, sad song high above the pathways of the sky. I thought of the marvel of creation, how all living things preyed on each other. Behind it the mystic eye of the Unseen Power who holds the world in the palm of His hand, directing its beams and beauty on the rich and the poor, on the just and the unjust.

CHAPTER 11

ONCE AGAIN bygone days flash back when I used to play with the neighbouring children at "housies", a game in which we imagined ourselves in possession of dwellings by the mere building up of a few stones, more or less in the form of a square, in which we placed tiny bits of broken coloured dishes and small stones by way of furniture, arranging and re-arranging, Tiring of that we played hide-and-seek, also a game of "tig". Eventually we sat down in the shade stringing daisy chains. The afternoon was fading, the shadows were beginning to lengthen and we were reminded it was seven o'clock, which meant bed-time. As I grew older I was allowed to stay up longer. I recall Auntie repeating many times to me, "Early to bed, early to rise, makes a man healthy, wealthy and wise". I can still hear the anxious voices of mothers calling their little ones home. They would go in search of them and draw them with exquisite tenderness into their arms. I would jerk myself away for the moment to control my agitation, feeling I ought not to be there, I did not belong to their world. I remember always that when I looked and watched them and looked away, I was compelled to look again. Somewhere in the depths of my being the picture struck a broken chord. My haphazard thoughts would wander back to a village. I saw a picture of myself brooding, full of sadness, always waiting — waiting in vain — for someone whose tender arms once held me close. Nobody living can escape the tragedy of separation. With the joy of companionship comes the fear that it must be lost as it must be at last. So I felt desperately lonely, broken and cast out into a wilderness, bereft of all save life itself. No one wanted a good for nothing brat. As I recall the reunion between mother and child, how I too, longed for a mother's loving clasp, which was denied me. I'm afraid I was inclined to sink too deep into an ocean of self pity. I would ponder within myself. Who was I? To whom did I belong? Why did they not want me? Those questions would revolve exhaustingly in my brain. Auntie Barbara could not be kinder, gifted with every womanly quality, but she was not my mother, and she was not my Auntie. As I look back I see how gently she treated me, how well she understood the state of my mind. What allowances she made for me! I can see what an undeveloped child I was, and what a woman she was, her patience, tolerance, her understanding and her gay manner, the building behind was strong and solid as the house she had been born in.

I cannot write this part without emotion as I gaze back across the years of my life. The picture of the cottage always remains with me. A dark wisp of smoke rises straight up from the chimney against the pale sky luminous with the pure light of morning that was strengthening with every minute. If I close my eyes and in the quiet of the moment quite close to me I hear a dear familiar sound of running water. I hear again the persistent sound of Auntie Barbara's voice, the eternal ticking of the old German clock on the mantelpiece, its chiming notes falling like pebbles into a clear pool. I can see again the polished steel fender round the glowing hearth, and the family Bible on the nearby shelf. There were the blue willow-pattern ashets and plates on the old-fashioned kitchen dresser. I listened to the gentle hum of the sewing machine as Auntie sat at the front room window stitching the garments. As I look back and remember some of the evenings spent with the happy group that formed round the fireside, where a friend was kindly treated and the stranger found himself at home, for seldom was the house without either, there would be fun and laughter, fireside stories and legends galore. One of the cottagers would play the melodeon, and they would sing their own haunting melodies and songs, I just remember two songs "Granny's Heilan Hame" and "The Crooked Bawbee", going right to the heart of the listener. One of the many favourite tunes played was "The Bonnie Lass of Bon Accord" Scott Skinner's favourite masterpiece. When ten o'clock chimed they prepared for departure. There would be goodnights, a hearty shake of the hands and a "haste ye back again" and made their way home by the light of the silvery moon. Auntie Barbara, unperturbed by the evening's uproar, would move quietly around putting her furniture back into place, smiling a little at some remembered incident.

Here, even in Summer, especially May and June there were gray, chilly wet days, the roads muddy and the trees dripping, bushes glittering with raindrops. But when the evening drew nigh, and however gloomy it would be, there was warmth and comfort inside. The satisfying earthy tang of the peats burning in the hearth, and the firelight making those framed pictures wink on the wall. In the stillness of the evening, Auntie would sit in her fire-side chair and talk of ordinary things and trivial incidents of the day. I've never known her to sit with her hands folded, for indeed she was always industrious — "Satan finds mischief for idle hands to do" she would quote to me, while I sat on my three legged-stool in a corner of the chimney piece with a slate and pencil struggling with my lessons. Eventually I finished up, torment-ing the drowsy cats, lying stretched out on the rug, their eyes opening slowly until two black orbs beamed on me. I would tickle their ears, and pull their whiskers, and make a dolly of one of them, sticking him in an old stocking, wind-ing a piece of rag round and round his body to keep him nice and firm and putting a wee toorie on his head. This reminds me of one of the Egyptian mummies lying in Marischal College Museum, Aberdeen. Now and then Auntie would stoke the fire up, the logs and peats falling into place and the flames roaring up the chimney. Later on, her eyes travelled to the clock. She would then pull the table near the fire and lay the supper. Usually I offered to help, but was told to sit down as I either upset or broke something. After supper Auntie prepared for bed, but before retiring would read a chapter and a psalm from the Book, as it was sometimes called (Bible). In my slippered feet Auntie with a lighted candle in her hand I scampered upstairs to bed, but dared not climb beneath the bedclothes until I knelt by the bedside and, under the watchful supervision of Auntie Barbara, repeated the Lord's Prayer, which she had taught me. She was eminently pious and much was I indebted to her kind guidance and christian admonition. One night, feeling rather mis-chievous I capered with the lighted candle, and set my flan-nelette nightdress on fire. Auntie, luckily having the presence of mind, threw something round my shoulders and clapped it out. My hair being in plaits, saved me from what might well have been a real tragedy.

I can still hear her scolding me, "What next will you be up to, you limmer?"

That night I was the most scared wee creature the world ever contained for all through the night I tossed and turned, thinking my nightdress was still on fire.

CHAPTER 12

IN THE mornings, Auntie was up with the lark, the fire on and the kettle singing, at eight o'clock she called me — not once, but half-a-dozen times — for I was really sleepy-headed in the mornings tumbling out of bed, rubbing the sleep from my eyes, I staggered downstairs to the fire, where my clothes were already heated and ready to wear. Then the fun started. I loathed having my face washed and my hair combed. "Och, the bagpipes have began" chaffed Auntie, at my tears. Eventually, I sat down to breakfast. Some of the scholars passing would give me a shout, oft-times I would jump up leaving my breakfast half finished and grab the milk pail, dash off to join them, shouting, "Wait for me, wait for me!", at the same time slinging my schoolbag over my shoulder I was still very much troubled with nose bleedings. It was nothing unusual to wake up in the morning to find my pillow saturated with blood. My chief ailments were headaches and sickness. Give the schoolmaster his due, he was most sympathetic if I wasn't feeling too well, and would send me home. Auntie would pilot me straight to bed and measure out a doze of castor-oil. You may be sure I pulled all sorts of faces, especially when she put it in milk. Every Saturday I got my usual dose of liquorice powder. It again was on the sweet side.

Looking back across the vista of years, remembering incidents which flit like shadows across my mind, I recall at sometimes or other in the garden eating hard gooseberries, when the stillness of the late afternoon was broken by Auntie Barbara's voice calling, "Lizzie, Lizzie". Peering through the bushes I answered, "I'm tasting the gooseberries, Auntie". "Mercy me, do you want to be sick? Come away at once, you mischief, or I'll take a stick to you", she called. I made off as fast as a rabbit, but no sooner had Auntie gone indoors then I was back again among the gooseberry bushes. Presently I began to feel queer, my tummy started to ache. Clutching myself round the waist, almost doubled up, I staggered into the house, howling and crying out, "Auntie, Auntie, my belly is sore". In a nettled tone of voice she replied, "Mahowker, (I don't care), it serves you right". Soon I was dealt with accordingly, given a dose of castor-oil and put to bed. Then the silvery haired Doctor England Kerr was telegraphed for. A tall, well built man, he had a most attractive smile, and a habit of raising one eyebrow. If I remember right he had a limp. Doctor Kerr came with all due haste in his old-fashioned two seater. I understand he was the first to own a car in Inverness. As he sat on the edge of my bed, he cracked jokes and gave me a few conundrums which I found somewhat cumbersome. One was, "Which is the heavier, a pound of gold or a pound of feathers?" You may be sure I said a pound of gold. My medicine arrived the following day by pony trap to Farr Post Office and delivered by Willie the postie. When Doctor Kerr visited me again, he brought me a basket of lovely ripe gooseberries. The postie, in those days, and still is, a sedate walker, and never lost sight of his feelings as a man in his position as a postie, Willie hardly missed a day without coming in for a smoke and a cup of tea. He was welcomed in every house in the Strath. He had a bicycle but it was more off the road than on. Willie had to travel unceasingly in all weathers. The Strath, in many parts, was very uninviting, even in the finest season. He had not the advantage of a regular road, but knowing all the localities he pushed his way even in darksome nights through hill and glen, fording the river and streams when they crossed his path. This last was one of his greatest perils, for the hill torrents came down so suddenly that we were often surprised at finding a flooded river and foot planks washed away when this was quite unlooked for, as I have already mentioned further back in my writing.

The folk on the Strath and outlying districts were mostly farmers and crofters, gamekeepers and shepherds, so on Saturdays, there was no want of employment or amusement to develop physical energy. The glorious out-door exercise over fields and moor was a joy to the boys and girls, and every season brought its own interesting work. The less fortunate in the Strath were wholly provided by the Laird. Old folks, widows and spinsters had their cottages or but-an-ben, sufficient ground to enable them to keep one cow or a goat, and raise potatoes and a small flower and vegetable garden, also kept hens and bees. The neighbouring farmers and crofters would help the less fortunate, carting home from the moss their peats to provide for warmth to tide them over the winter months. Between seven and eight o'clock on Sunday mornings, surrounded by a wealth of summer, it was a peaceful leisurely scene and most touching to see the old folk and youngsters sitting here and there by the roadside or by some bridle path in a tunnel of deep green where the trees over-arched, herding their cows, which were contentedly grazing the grass, dandelions and flowering growth and flicking their tails over their glossy nut-brown hides. To those humble folk the cow was another human being, one of the family. It was nothing unusual for Auntie Barbara to open the door in the morning to find a jug of warm milk and crowdie on the doorstep. In summer, when the tempo of things slow down, the countryside still hums with movement all day and every day. In the clear morning air, I would hear the sounds of a wakening world, the faint sounds of life, from afar came the sound of sheep, dogs and shepherds and shouting. From somewhere a man's hammering as he repaired a fence where some restive horses may have kicked a hole, or sheep may have opened a gap in the wire, and nearby workmen busy resurfacing the road with stones that had hitherto been broken by hand with a hammer, and not far away the forest echoes to the blows of the woodcutters axe as he chips around the base of the tree trunk before using the crosscut saw.

Once again my memory strays to the ever changing rhythm of country life speaking strong but simple, I can hear the brisk trot of hooves and the clink of harness as the farm carts rumble past. The sound of a lad whistling the "Highland Cradle Song" comes down from a hillside byre. On Tuesday and Friday mornings come carts and pony traps swaying and jolting on their way down to the market, carrying their home produce, eggs, kebbocks of cheese, crowdie and fresh churned butter, wrapped in cabbage leaves, protected by old tarpaulin covers. On market days there is always an undercurrent of excitement, The entrances from Union Street and Church Street and the entrances from Academy Street and Queensgate to the market alive with activity. And beyond Eastgate the mart, full of big picturesque-looking men with long flowing beards, with their equally picturesque Highland cattle.

There were greetings, bits of gossip, keen bargains, and a dram or two. From somewhere around the pibroch is sounding and resounding. Inverness, the capital of the Highlands, with all its confusion of tartans, for nowhere beats the heart so kindly as beneath the tartan plaid. Inverness is charmingly situated at the head of the Moray Firth and at the north-eastern end of the Great Glen which contains the Caledonian Canal. It is a well built town. Through it flows, like the curves of a lady's leg, the clear and rapid River Ness, dividing it into two unequal portions, the larger being on the eastern bank. The river is spanned by five bridges while in the background far away on the north west, is massive Ben Wyvis which rises to a height of rather less than 3500 feet. To the south west of the Great Glen is Ben Nevis rising to a height of 4406 feet. Ben Wyvis and Ben Nevis stand by like sentinels with the solemn grandeur and beauty which are theirs at all times. The sweet scent of past yesterdays is with me again. The guardians of the soil would return home tired but happy, laden with farm implements and bulging with household goods. On darker nights a fixed head-lamp on their machines and carts lit the roadway in front of their path and swinging lanterns at the rear cast grotesque shadows round about.

CHAPTER 13

AS I grew older Auntie Barbara, at the weekends, set me to perform small tasks and run errands. On Tuesdays and Fridays a grocery van from Inverness provided the Strath with groceries, but for all that, we still went short of something or other. So with a wheel of an old bicycle, which we children called a gird, and guiding it with a stick, I would be gone with the wind, racing along the everchanging country-side until I reached Farr Post Office which was also a General Store and sold more or less a little of everything including paraffin for the lamps. When they were short of supplies, especially bread, weather permittimg, the assistant would harness the horse to the pony-trap and drive to Inverness.

On Saturdays there were a hundred and one things to be done when preparing for the next day, Sunday, so after breakfast there were hens to be fed, eggs to be collected, wood to be gathered for kindling the fire and cart enough water in pails from the pump which was about two hundred yards away, to keep us going till Monday morning. While I carried out those simple tasks, Auntie would collect her cleaning paraphernalia, and flit from room to room, her mountainous skirts hissing as though they housed beneath their folds a colony of serpents, sweeping and dusting and straightening her furniture — a job at which I was hopeless. When trying to sweep the floor, I shoved dust under the mat or in to a corner. Auntie Barbara wouldn't see me in her way, and chaffed me, saying I was more bother than all the worth of me. Besides I thought house-brooms were beastly things, I preferred to be out of doors where allurements were stronger. I recall Auntie quoting to me "Where there's a will there's a way".

I recall one Saturday Alick Smith, a neighbour, saying to me "Liz, I wish you would go and fetch Nanny home (the goat)". "Where is she?" I asked. "Oh, she's away being served at Balnafoich Farm". I informed Auntie that I was about to run an errand for Alick Smith but did not tell her the nature of it. I headed for the farm, which lay about three miles east the road. As I climbed Balnafoich Brae, I saw Mr Ferguson, the farmer, in the yard and approached him some- what gingerly and explained I had come to take Nanny home. He looked at me dubiously, stroking his chin. then grinned. I had to convince him I was in deadly earnest, and that Nanny knew me. As my eye roved around, I spotted her grazing not far from the Billy Goat. I called to her and she lifted up her head and gave a bleat and bounded forward to greet me. Without any further ado, Mr Ferguson tied a bit of stack rope round her neck and we set off for home. Now and again she would start showing off, going through a series of antics, prancing, jumping and standing on her hind legs and lowering her head to butt, as if she was putting on an act for my benefit, all it needed now was a flock of goosey ganders from the farm yard to bring up the rear. When we came to Farr Post Office, some of the local folk started behaving in a teasing manner and saying "There are two goats now". I took it all in good part, letting it in one ear and out the other. What a surprise Alick and the wife got when Nanny and I entered the living room. He told me he was only pulling my leg and never dreamed for a moment I would take him seriously, but, for all that. Alick and the wife were glad to have her back safe and sound.

Gradually an interest in the garden kindled within me, so most of the evenings were spent in cleaning the jungle of weeds from the potatoes and adding earth, also weeding the flower-beds and paths. I regarded the weeds as "Old Nick's Family" for they sprouted up in spite of me, and I would have to start all over again and bestow order, tidying up the confusion that confronted me. Often in summer, Mother Earth would be almost sunbaked, her multitude of crops and plants drooping for the want of rain, especially the young cabbages. In the evenings I would be forced to draw water from the burn, which bound the west-side of the house, where a break in the bank revealed stepping stones down to the edge, which once had been a muddy slope. Trudging back and fore watering the plants kept me busy till bed-time.

From an open window of a nearby cottage comes the sound of a record being played on an old fashioned gramophone — "His Master's Voice". As I lifted my head I could hear the sweet musical voice of Dame Clara Butt rising higher and higher as she sang "Within a mile of Edinburgh toon in the rosy time of the year." I just remember a few words which I didn't understand then, they were, "I canna canna, winna winna, manna buckle tae". Now and again I caught a glimpse of the swallow as he or she skimmed high above the roof top and suddenly disappeared into its wee housie beneath the eaves. The swallow reminds me of that song, La Golandrina.

To distant climbs the swallow now is fleeting
For sharp's the breath that warns of summers flown
On dauntless wing she soars and with her passing
My musing heart recalls fond scenes long known.

Sleep came without rocking till I woke with the dawn on the pane to the everlasting wonder of trees, birds, beasts and flowers.

CHAPTER 14

JULY SWEEPS in, aglow with summer brilliance, lay in a picturesque confusion as bright as some of Auntie Barbara's coloured scenes that hung on the kitchen walls. For with the month of July comes our school holidays. I remember Mrs MacKenzie of Farr presenting us with our prizes and entertaining us on the front lawn of Farr House, her household staff at our disposal. The sports were held in the park beside Farr Loch. One year we were shepherded in to two horse drawn carriages and driven over twenty miles by Daviot passing

Moy Hall, the Ancestral home of the MacKintosh of Mac-Kintosh. According to our history, Bonnie Prince Charlie when a fugitive, sought shelter there. Down came Lady MacKintosh and opened wide the gate. I recall stopping by the wayside, resting and feeding the horses, then after a snack of biscuits and cheese, we continued our journey to Glen-mazeran, one of Mr and Mrs MacKenzie's Estates, where we were entertained. Returning home in the late afternoon, I remember we passed the River Findhorn, and took the short-cut and followed the narrow winding track through the hills called Creag-na-Gobhair, some of us had to get down and open two or three gates and shut them again. Those hills are not very high but there is something in their shape and the steepness with which they rise, which gives an impression of overpowering mass. We climbed laboriously for seven and three-quarter miles, the carriages jolted and bumped. Half way home, one of the horses gave up and we all had to scramble in to one carriage, squashed like sardines in a tin. Every dusty mile brought us nearer home, and before we knew it we had climbed the last brae. Gazing down we saw the whole Strath in a clear and lovely light — sharp, agonising beauty. The scene went straight to my heart. Mr and Mrs MacKenzie have since then passed on. A nephew Major Alexander MacKenzie, was now the new Laird.

During the summer holidays, I was able to help with the blanket washing which took place sometime in July. One of the neighbours would come and give us a helping hand. It doesn't take long to light a fire, when you have dry twigs from an old fir tree, the crackle and roar became a blazing cone and here we used an out-sized iron pot to heat the water, treading with our bare feet was the usual process. Two of us would trample together in the same wooden tub, with one arm encircling each other's waist frequently changing our arms, as we moved in a contrary direction. The light of the sun was fading as we put an end to our labours, Auntie Barbara would have a cheery fire and a hot supper ready,

Moy Hall

Inverness Fun Run, 22nd July 1984

perhaps a stewed rabbit or a pot-roasted chicken, potatoes dressed in their jackets or floury waistcoats, girdle scones and oatcakes fresh off the brander, home-made jam, etc, lovely creamy milk, not forgetting tea. It never tasted so good, as it did after some of those heavy washings. Later in the evening when I retired for the night I pondered over the day's experience and, with a sigh of contentment, I blew out the candle and sank into a blessed sleep until the crowing of the cock heralded the approaching dawn and a faint ghostly light over the east.

CHAPTER 15

EVERY SUMMER Eastern Cottage became a peaceful guest-house over a period of four weeks. One of the guests was a Miss Jessie MacBean, who was a sister of Mr John MacBean, Poor Inspector, Inverness, and her devoted companion, Mrs Fraser, both Invernessians. Sometimes Miss MacBean's sister, Anna, would join them on a weekend. Miss Jessie MacBean suffered from the effects of rheumatic fever, and had to have the support of two walking sticks. She spent most of her time sitting in the shade of the veranda. She was kindness itself, always fresh and cheery. She possessed courage and a keen sense of humour and kept interests alive with her zest for life to the end. I recall one day playing a practical joke. Taking the stairs two at a time, I clambered out through one of the bedroom windows and slithered down the roof of the veranda lying flat on my stomach. I peeped out the edge of the rhone and let out a terrific "boo!" giving poor Miss MacBean the scare of her life, crying out, "You can't catch me!" She shook her stick vindictively, which I thought was great fun and I burst out into fits of merriment. She was equally as good as Auntie Barbara at calling me a limmer, woe betide me if I came within reach of her. Then suddenly I heard Auntie's voice bringing a domestic note into the scene, "Come off that roof at once, you limmer" three times she called: Closing up like an oyster I gingerly crawled back the way I came, going head first through the window, landing with a thud on the floor, a little out of breath, disarrayed and scratched, At meal times I was "Sssh'd" into obedience, "Little girls ought to be seen and not heard".

I remember one Sunday morning at ten o'clock the chimney went on fire. I heard the crackling grow louder and fiercer as the fire fastened its tenacious fingers about the chimney and became one thunderous roar, throwing everyone into a panic. Heat from the hearth blew in waves across my face, fumes blinding my eyes, stinging them to wetness: Outside belching smoke and tongues of flame leapt high in the air each passing moment increasing its volume: Showers of sparks flew in all directions like fireworks. I ran about getting in folk's way, terrified out of my wits, as part of my child's mind saw a picture of the house burnt, and not having anywhere to go. Auntie, with the help of the neighbours, and poor Mrs Fraser helping, feverishly swept up the fiery cinders that came rumbling down the chimney and shooting across the floor leaving their marks printed indelibly on the linoleum. Water was thrown on to the burning hearth. Slowly the roar ceased, but the chimney still smouldered until four o'clock in the afternoon. It was with profound relief that we saw it die out silently and we all relaxed over a cup of tea our next door neighbour had brought in. The scene was one never to be forgotten. The chimney solution was to select three or four slender lengths of rowan of fair strength and much flexibility, lay them on the ground all facing one way, placing each length behind the previous one, making them secure. We then tied a piece of brush-wood or heather at the thin end. This was the sweeping brush. If it was too long to fit into the room, we just let it in from the front door and curved it up the chimney, brushing as we heaved it little by little, taking precaution to wear an old coat and hat.

CHAPTER 16

MY THOUGHTS go back happily to picnics as if it were yesterday. I set out on a cloudless July morning arranging to join Mr MacGillivray, the game-keeper and his wife and family at the boathouse beside Farr Loch, a favourite venue, we helped to push the boat down the shingle into the water, surrounded by water lilies dancing up and down like nymphs.

Farr Loch lay amethystine for a mile long. Amidst shouts and laughter and the rattle of goods and chattels, we scrambled into the boat almost capsizing her in our enthusiasm as we pushed out onto the loch. Pulled by sturdy rowers, we swept along, drinking in the magnificent grandeur of Highland scenery — the sound of our voices echoing and re-echoing through the hills as we sang "Speed Bonnie Boat". Now and again we glimpsed a trout glittering in the sunlight as it leapt high above the surface. It was truly wonderful! The loch shone like a mirror spread out to catch the blush of a new-born day. Across its pathways came the clear call of the cuckoo, while along its margin thickly wooded, the branches were reflected on the surface, and the beauty of the Kingfisher as he skimmed across quiet waters. We rowed to the upper end and moored the boat to an old tree trunk. Here we were free to sport and play. There was the excitement of gathering wood to build a fire, while I went off to fill a kettle from a gurgling stream. How beautiful was the sound as the water sang and danced by my feet. We picnicked under the shadows of some trees, we sat down and partook of the feast. I can assure you we ate it heartily. Then began the sky-larking, paddled through every pool and rolled ourselves among the heather, pranced and capered. We pelted one another with harmless material, but we used more gentle methods than those practised at school. When wearied we lay down in some sheltered nook, where all was quiet and silent. This was not to last long for it was presently broken by a shout as one of the boys who had wandered off now came back, a sparkle in his eye. He had spotted a roebuck which had strayed from the herd. We gave chase. There she was on the steep slope of a summit, white spotted, her antlers like the antlers of a stag, and it was just as well for us to try and catch "The Pride and Terror of the Glen" (The Golden Eagle). We returned from vain pursuits. Time went by unnoticed. We children who adventure will always know the depths, and if chance should offer a track which takes us off our beat, we try it venturing the heights and although we must return home we are always the richer for the memory. Yes, we were a happy party. Thus it went on until late afternoon, full of whoops and shrieks. Pleasantly tired after a day's excitement, we packed up and wound our way down to the boat where the waves were gently lapping her sides. As we sped homeward bound, it was an enchanted evening of great beauty with a little breeze from the west. The glowing sun was high above the horizon. Slowly the spark of red was quenched in the waters of the Loch. The hills were aglow with purple light. Slowly the sun dipped for a few seconds, the hills continued to glow, which then went out, leaving them like wan ghosts.

CHAPTER 17

THE SABBATH in the Strath was much observed as a day of worship. Auntie Barbara was a member of a small denomination called "Free Presbyterians" or Seceders. As there was no resident Clergyman in the Strath, the Sunday services were conducted by a missionary or an Elder from the town who had, for many years, been weekend guests of Miss Cameron, Post Mistress at Farr Post Office. The old schoolhouse at Dalavourn which was used as a church, was about two miles east along the road. A cart track wound its way to where it was situated on the moor, sheltered by a few trees. Once a fortnight the Sunday evening services were held in

Auntie Barbara's house, for the aged and infirm living near-by. Auntie would clear the kitchen of the smaller furniture. Wooden forms and chairs were arranged round the room and the Gaelic Bible was placed on a small table by the fireside, and a glass of water stood on a near-by shelf for old Mr Bannerman with which to quench his thirst. He was over seventy years of age. Auntie would receive the people with quiet composure and the comparative warmth of the fire and frankincense pouring from pyramids of logs and peats welcomed them. If I remember rightly the service started at seven o'clock. The Sermon was first preached in Gaelic then translated into English. Seated, they began with the singing of a psalm, a little out of tune. Then came a prayer, which I thought was never going to end. The two oldest members who attended the service were Mary MacPherson, eighty years of age and old Sandy MacPhail, over ninety years old. Sandy, incidentally, lived to the ripe old age of a hundred and two or three.

Once a year in July they held their Communion. I recall one of those Sundays. It was a day of perfect summer glory. All roads and tracks from the Strath and outlying parishes were astir, journeying from as far as Dingwall, Inverness, Errogie and Stratherrick. Old women, dressed in their mutches tied with black ribbons. Auntie Barbara's mutch was also black tied with a broad black ribbon in a bow beneath her chin, and clothes of old decency and adornments smelling like moth balls; they were never taken out of the kist, except on such occasions as the present, or for a family marriage, feast or funeral. The people collected in groups greeting each other with warmth and a hearty shake of the hand. Mr Mac-Queen, their minister, and Elders moved about conversing with them. The weather being perfect, Holy Communion was celebrated out of doors. A long, narrow table like a bench, covered with a white cloth, was placed near a hillock sheltered by a few trees, The Communicants were seated on each side while the rest of the congregation arranged themselves round about, sitting on stones and bunches of heather. Most touching it was to hear their voices raised in harmony, singing the hundred and twenty-first psalm; slow, solemn and sweet to the ears of those who understood, rolling across the broken moorland in wave after wave. That night the sun went down in full splendour. A most touching and memorable scene. Years later a church was built a little way up the back road, behind Farr Post Office.

CHAPTER 18

LETTING MY mind run back to the past, I see myself, a little lassie, running west the road, passing Achnabeachan Farm, which belonged to Jimmy MacBain and had been in his family since 1876. Jimmy was a sniper in the First World War. There is no-one there now, all have passed on. Bordering the land on the left hand side of the road, for nearly a mile, there is a fine birch wood. The trees were in their summer dress of tender green. In Autumn their leaves turn to orange and flaming gold, and there is sometimes a flash of red among the birches as a Woodpecker flits through the trees, as I sped along the roadside dotted here and there with Rowan trees, their branches like the fiery tongues of Penticost.

Suddenly I saw the house where Auntie Barbara was born, Sockich, huddled down below the road out of the wind. It nestles in a grassy valley through which flows the River Nairn, In my mind's eye I saw children here, lots of them. They were Auntie Barbara's relatives, also boarded out children, all running in and out of the house with its sunny old-fashioned garden, where flowers, fruit and vegetables were mixed together. Often I would join them, but as soon as I showed myself one of the family would greet me by saying, "Here you are, Nurse MacKay", and thrust a baby into my arms to nurse, or the wooden cradle to rock on the uneven stone-flagged floor. Appetising smells of cooking would come from the pots that hung from the swivel over the peat fire which was a slab of stone called the hearth and the black iron kettle always on the boil and the brown earthenware teapot beside the fire. Seated on a stoolie I would sing lullabies coaxing the baby to sleep.

On the other side of the River Nairn, are the ruins of Glen Nairn, once the scene of continued peace and comfort, the happy home of the Ross family and around it the green sward and marks of cultivation are still to be seen. The Ross's and the boarded out children including myself played together, We would call to one another from across the river, our voices echoing and re-echoing betwixt valley and glen — "We're coming over to play", while the group on the opposite side would wave back. In a flash, with the sure-footedness of a young roebuck, we would career over the cobbled stones, past the byre, down a footpath between the fields and over the narrow footplank, a late comer would splash through the river, and race across the warren, almost buried in bracken, shouting and waving, "I'm coming too. Wait for me, wait for me".

I recall evenings when Auntie Barbara, with me clinging to her skirt travelled west to Sockich, under the magic canopy of stars and the whole Strath bathed in moonlight, which turned it into an enchanted fairy land. There would be a good houseful of folk, with Archie playing the melodeon, "The Barren Rocks of Aden" and a number of other tunes and Strathspeys. After an enjoyable evening and a bit gossip, not forgetting a well-laid table, we made our way home. Here and there what looked like glow-worms proved to be gleams of steady lights from the farms and cottages, while the air was drugged with peat reek from their firesides.

Next came berry picking. The afternoon found me saddled with a basket engaged in picking the blackcurrants from the bushes at the back of the house and along the garden fence, I'm afraid more went into my mouth than into the basket. When detected by Auntie Barbara, I would say, "I

43

don't know how it comed there". The mispronounciation of the word became quite a joke with Auntie and I was to dense to see it. One day I went further afield to gather wild rasps, seemingly they were sweeter than the garden ones and made better jam. I wandered off the beaten track to where they were more plentiful. Leaning too far over, I balanced dangerously, slipped and slithered down the steep incline in among some bramble bushes. I do declare I thought I sat on a hedgehog and what with nettles and one thing and another adding to the tangled confusion and with hands sorely scratched by the vicious pricks, somewhat out of patience, I struggled until the last strands were severed from my clothes. When I arrived home I kept quiet about my catastrophe for fear of Auntie teasing me, "Och, it wouldn't be you unless you got yourself into some pickle". I was far from being comfortable when I sat down and kept fidgeting. Auntie, noticing my restlessness, chaffed me, saying, "Mercy me, anyone to see you would think you had pins and needles in your bottom". She wasn't far wrong.

CHAPTER 19

THE SUMMER passed, August arrived in a haze of quivering gold. Her breath was warm with the golden redness of the misty Autumn. The whole farmer's world would be bustling. Out of the cob-webbed shadows came the reapers and the binders to be over-hauled. The fields, which have been quiet, echo to the noise of harvesters. On the small crofts the scythe is used. In the evenings I raced along to Sockich and joined the happy throng, giving them a helping hand at gathering the corn. We made the bands and tied the sheaves, while some of us followed picking them up by the long side and stood them upright with the shorter side inwards so that they naturally leaned together keeping the whole stook standing firmly. If the sheaves were in any way damp we left them to air before setting them up. After a few days, each boasted a pitch-fork, we whipped the sheaves smartly from the stooks and tossed them to the lads above, to be carted away to the stackyard to be built into stacks. The folk in the Strath, who were very good forecasters of any change to be in the weather, shaped the day accordingly and often worked well into the evenings, bringing their corn home by the light of the harvest moon. In extra times of stress they would come to each other's rescue and sometimes the harvest days lasted far into September. You can imagine the fun we youngsters had when the last load was carted off to the stackyard, our ghostly figures streaking across the empty field, stripped of its harvest, playing tick-tack in and out of the corn stacks, amidst screams and shrills ringing far into the night until we were hustled off to bed. Goodnights and a wave of the hand, I was gone, home to roost.

I have seen the seasons fashion their changes over this land which was once home. Hills beyond hills, until cloud and country mingle, with all their vivid lights and shadows, the lonely hills and moors covered with heather, bent bracken and bog-myrtle which makes the air fragrant with scents and provides a home for grouse, partridge, pheasant and through which hinds and stags leap with amazing speed. A glorious panorama of natural beauty which baffles description, A happy hunting ground for the sportsman. With the approach of the "Glorious Twelfth," all roads lead to the Highlands.

Then came the potato harvest, followed by a dinner and dance given by Mr and Mrs MacKenzie of Farr, held in Farr Dance Hall, with its spacious floor, its walls adorned with stags heads. Each and all were invited, down to the last but-an-ben and all sitting down at the same table, the Laird and his Lady at the head, After we had partaken of a good feast and the best of wine and as soon as the swift lilting tinkle of sound started, dancing commenced. Seated all round about, young and old, we were like a family gathering, for everybody knew everybody else, it was great fun, mingling with the dancers amidst hoochs and skirls and most a enjoyable evening. This was the traditional end to a happy toil.

CHAPTER 20

THE SCHOOL holidays would suddenly come to an end, once more back to that school of learning. I saw myself, a little lassie, hurrying off to school, catching up on my school mates coming to Milton brae. I turned in at the gate leading to Farr Mains, where I deposited the milk pail outside the dairy door. sometimes grazing nearby there would be a herd of pedigree shaggy Highland Cattle with their horns spanning over four feet, bred on Farr Estate. I recall Mr Mathieson, the manager, showing me one with horns that spanned over five feet.

Beside the farm stood the Old Meal Mill which held a strange fascination for me. Its massive machinery, big wheels and broad belts turning and twisting. The noise was something deafening, one could not hear oneself speaking. It was here that the guardians of the soil brought their oats to be ground down into meal. Once a year some of the old folk would come for fresh chaff to renew their beds. I always had the feeling that chaff beds harboured fleas.

Beside the Meal Mill was the sawmill used by the Estate workers for sawing the lengths of tree trunks into planks, used for building purposes, gates and posts for the fences, near by stood a large tank containing Cuprinol diluted with water was used for seasoning the wood.

On our way to school we sometimes met a fisherman from Inverness with a little pony and cart on his way west the country selling herrings. I remember Auntie Barbara getting twelve for a penny. On his way back if he hadn't sold them all, he would dump them somewhere along the roadside rather than take them back into town. We scholars had to keep a sharp look-out for fear of slithering in among them, which wouldn't be the first time.

The first day at school our names would be called out, also there would be a few young beginners, increasing the number of pupils to well over thirty. I recall us having our photograph taken, but I'm afraid half of the scholars didn't turn up. There was only nineteen with Mr MacRae, the schoolmaster, in the group. Alick MacKenzie, first on the left in the front row, in later years became the chief reporter of the "People's Journal" in Inverness. Johnnie Fraser, the boy in the front row beside the Master became a minister and myself on the left in the second row, with a face like a dried herring. The photograph was taken by a Mr Fleming from Inverness, in the year 1920.

When playtime came, instead of getting right down to our games and outrageous fights for a while we would play at hares and hounds in the plantation beside the school. We girls being the hares and the boys the hounds who gave chase. Tiring of that and in spite of a slight drizzle, we would climb over the school dyke and race across the heather clad moor and hold our faces up to feel the rain like needles on our cheeks, breathing in the pure air, sweet with fragrant odours, then we would have a game of hide and seek among the stone boulders dotted here and there. There was one just outside the school gate which we sometimes used as a chute, wearing the seat out of our bloomers which was the term used in those days. After that we would take a flying leap from the bank over the fence, down a steep incline, going helter-skelter to the edge of the River Fearorach, a tributary of the River Nairn which flowed past below the school. Off would come our boots and stockings. Here we shrieked and splashed one another until the shrill blast of the Master's whistle, once again, reminded us our playtime was up. Being the first day, after our holidays, we got home earlier.

On the way I would call in at Farr Post Office to collect Auntie Barbara's pension, if I remember right it was either five shillings or seven and sixpence. Eventually, it went up to ten shillings a week. While in the shop, old Mr Cameron, with a piece of paper, would make a poke and fill it with sweets for me. As I hurried along the road and went in at the bottom gate leading to Farr Mains, before collecting the milk pail, I would pop into see old Jock the Miller, who would greet me, "Well, little wifie, have you come to see me?" I would help him to stoke up the furnace throwing on firewood and shovelling in chaff. Before leaving he would fill my pockets with toasted corn taken from the furnace room, or kiln before being ground into oatmeal, which was very good to eat, a diet in itself. When working as house table-maid in Doctor Murray's, 6 Ardross Terrace, Inverness, the cook/ housekeeper, a Miss Maggie MacLeod told me she was a close friend of the mother of the MacDonald brothers of the Maison Victoria, Academy Street, inventors of the Mac-Donald steam system of permanent waving. When studying in London, the Professor asked them what they fed their brains on in Scotland. They answered "Brose". They did not forget they were matured on oatmeal.

CHAPTER 21

I REMEMBER one of those glorious yesterdays, I roamed down the bridle path at the east side of the house passing old Mill Cottage through a labyrinth clothed with translucent leaves, skirting old Mary MacPherson's but-an-ben and down a steep track through the wood which led to the moor. My heart sang with joy as I danced on my way, touching the leaves and pendant tassels, chanting a melody, the twittering of the birds, the cooing of the male wood pigeons in the heavy foliage and squirrels rippled from one hazel to another like wind fanned flames. Huge corpses of tree trunks sprawled on the ground, their limbs like broken arms of giant men, their fingers gripping the earth, lying where they fell through the weight of years, with the violence of storm. It was like coming upon a scene of a skirmish waged long ago. One could imagine they heard the battle cries of a colourful confusion of clans mingling with the skirl of the bag-pipes. Their kilts and plaids swinging as they charged down the steep hillside fording the rivers and streams, the glitter of steel and the clang of sword and shield rank upon rank of the country's heroes as they grappled with the enemy. Somewhere in the midst is a fair young man, the "Young Pretender" seeking a Crown which his grandfather James II lost for his illustrious race. The heather clad bosom of Mother Earth stained with blood, shudders beneath the bodies of the dead and the groans of the wounded seem to echo across the rugged hills and moors, casting a spell of bygone glory over all. I recall Auntie Barbara saying that Bonnie Prince Charlie passed through Strathnairn hidden in a load of hay and took refuge for the night in Tordarroch farm house, some distance at the back of Farr Post Office over the humpy backit brae.

As I came to the edge of the wood, I crossed over a very creaky wobbly footbridge spanning the River Nairn. I found myself walking in the direction of Dunlichity an ancient Parish, united in 1618 to Daviot. It takes its name originally from Dunlecatti signifying "Hill of Cattle" from a hill adjacent to its church. The church was rebuilt in 1758 and contains three hundred sittings. The Catti whose territory lay in and around it, were the ancestors of the Clan Chattan, comprising Mac-Kintoshs, MacPhersons, MacKays, Camerons, Davidsons, MacGillivrays, Smiths and others. I recall once attending a Sunday Service in the Church. It so happened that Mr MacLean, the Parish Minister at Daviot, who conducted the services, was ill and unable to come and an old minister from some other Parish officiated. I cannot recall the text, but I do remember this episode. Gazing up into the minister's face, feeling very serious, while he ranted and thumped with his fist, swaying in the pulpit, crouching, then raising himself again and again to his full height, he suddenly thrust himself forward catapulting those words over the heads of the congregation — "Some people come to hear the latest news, others come to hear the price of coos". There were titterings everywhere, I just exploded, trying to smother my giggle and almost choking on a peppermint which I was sucking. I glanced sideways and saw Mr MacRae, my schoolmaster, sitting at my back. There was a smile beneath his moustache and a glint in his dark eyes. I was mighty thankful when the service ended, for once outside along with some of the local children, we gave vent to shrieks and laughter, for indeed I could have told him that some people came to close their eyes, while others came to eye the clothes.

Scrambling up the hill and on to the track, I walked a short distance and climbed over the dyke of the cemetery, cared for by old Donald Forbes. I wandered among the moss-covered tombs and inspected the weathered stones marking the last resting place of Highland Kinsmen. The oldest stone was marked 1707.

Sitting down, I propped myself against the little old "Watch Tower" remembering Auntie Barbara telling me that in the early part of the eighteenth century, body snatching in the Highlands was by no means uncommon. Some of the local folk, including Auntie Barbara's father, Archibald Fraser, Sockich, often watched for ten days or so after a funeral. There was, in most graveyards a small watch tower where the watch was kept. In this little building the watchers had a fire, some refreshments and an old gun. A slab of stone was used as a target to scare the traffickers. The latter, of course, could expect little mercy when caught red-handed in the act of desecrating a grave. The marks of the bullets and pellets on the stone surface are still to be seen. It was the business of the men to follow and spy in some way on every funeral and then at night creep out and open the new grave, burst open the lid, strip the corpse and carry it off wrapped in sacking to some surgeon for his dissecting table to further the advance in the field of surgery. As I sat leaning against the old watch tower, it made me shiver when I thought about those stealthy creatures burrowing into the earth like foxes, their hands tearing the shrouds from new buried bodies. You can imagine their hard breathing and their starts at every sound. It brings to mind one of Auntie Barbara's stories of a woman travelling to Inverness who was overtaken by a cart, occupied by two or three men and was offered a lift. The woman was most grateful and thanked them kindly. But nearing the town she chanced to look round and noticed a toe protruding from underneath a tarpaulin which on closer examination formed the outlines of a human body. The woman felt much startled but had the presence of mind not to show in any way whatsoever that she suspected such a thing as a corpse being in the cart. Every Highlander will remember stories and legends to which in his youth he listened, while one of a circle sitting by the fireside. This tale is about a certain churchyard in some out-lying parish. A party was arranging flowers on a relative's grave when their attention was arrested by the figure of a man in evening clothes moving with the silent swiftness of a ghost over the graveyard until he came to a grave, from which, to their amazement, they saw a sheeted figure of an old man with a long hoary beard, rise up and shake hands with the person just come, after which they separated, the gentleman in his evening clothes returning as he came and the shrouded one to his earthly cell below. The story goes that the dressed gentleman was dying in some far off land and his image appeared in the graveyard and that his last wish was to be laid beside the person whose bones tenanted the grave.

I recall another of Auntie Barbara's stories. This incident happened many years ago, about a minister, the Rev. Mr Cook, who was called to conduct the service at Daviot Parish Church. When visiting his parishoners, he travelled on horseback as some of them lived in very remote parts. Sometime after one of those visits he received word to visit a man who was dying in some out-lying district. The man told him how he and his companion were waiting along the lonely track to take his life, rob him and take his horse, but suddenly in the distance they saw two other figures of men on horseback one on each side of him and it baffled them, so he asked the minister, "Who were the other two with you?" The minister said there was nobody with him, he was quite alone. It surely must have been his Guardian Angels protecting him.

I felt a chill in the air and rose scrambling over the dyke. My eyes travelled to the west of Dunlichity, towards Loch Duntelchaig which supplies Inverness with water, piped into Loch Ashie. There, among the hills in April and May, a natural rock garden very bright with flowers, the yellow of the broom and the yellow of the primroses blending with the deep blue of wild violets and the white of wood anemones, from somewhere around comes the sound of running water taking its unknown course. I should not like to be alone there at the moment of twilight, when hills step forward in the clearness of the air: For in the eerie silence we glimpse the land of legend. A mist was creeping along like a monster rising out of the deep, to me there is something ghostly about mist and as I looked the shroud enfolded the valley. I began to remember stories about people who had been overtaken by mist on the moors and had been found a few days later huddled in the heather, dead from exposure. I remember, too, with a creeping chill, here amidst the lonely hills, the witch who haunted the moors and desolate places, whose appearance invariably heralded calamity, and who could turn herself into any shape. Later she was caught by a shepherd and his two dogs in the shape of a hare, and burnt in a barrel of tar on Brin Estate, three miles west from Dunlichity.

Speaking about Brin Estate remindes me of a Saturday afternoon when all my chores were done and with permission from Auntie Barbara to join some of my schoolmates on a ramble, our footsteps led us to Brin Rock on Stuart's of Brin's Estate which is several hundred feet above sea level, brightened up with waving green trees scattered here and there on its steep slope. All of a sudden we dared one another to scale the rock. After much argument, we agreed, the oldest leading the way while the rest of us followed suit full of expectation; we imagined ourselves belonging to an expeditionary force. The going was tough as we hauled ourselves up with the aid of shrubs and roots and footholds created by nature, frequently stopping to rest. The rock looked so dark and formidable, a fall would have proved disastrous. Eventually we succeeded in reaching the top triumphantly but, alas, quite unlooked for, we encountered a herd of untamed goats, cutting short our exploration. They seemed to resent our entry into their domain, making threatening gestures of head lowering, and as we weren't equipped to meet in combat we turned tail, making a quick descent amidst yells and screams, slithering down, somebody shouting, "Och, I've torn my breeks" another "Oh, I've got a stab in my bum". As for myself, my bloomers got caught on an over-hanging branch leaning on the slope: some of them had to edge back up and free me. We reached the bottom scratched and dishevelled and a little out of breath. It was a memory of an adventure that we would not soon forget.

Other and stranger tales would crowd into my mind. According to an old legend told to me by Auntie Barbara, some children wandering on the banks of a pond near Brin School were attracted by a beautiful horse which rose out of the water. Its main object was to entice human beings into the water with himself. They were tempted to touch it and when the horse started to withdraw itself they discovered they could not free themselves. One little boy, realising his predicament, took his pocket knife and somehow freed himself, just as the tempter plunged beneath the depths.

As I picked my way home, hoping for the mist to lift, I looked back and saw the little church nestling among the trees and the old watch tower showing grey against the green foliage, standing guard over the tombs of loved ones, the long dead ones and the newly dead, with the moss covered stones of old inhabitants whose inscriptions are seldom more than a statistical table of birth and death. I turned away and stumbled into patches of bog, slipping on bits of heather, and began to feel uneasy as a hill sheep started in terror almost at my feet. I could hear it bolting away and then a startled bird would suddenly fly into the mist with a whirring sound. At such a time imagination grows, unusual and unwanted shapes and eerie sounds are created by mist and clouds among the awful solitudes of nature which always has the laugh on man and cannot be tamed. My thoughts were so full of superstition that I gave a start to find that the mist had suddenly lifted and the sun had burst forth in full splendour from behind the dark mist that had hitherto obscured its rays. As I looked the house loomed ahead and a dark twist of smoke rose from its chimney. I felt a glow of warmth kindle within me, for indeed, to me there is no place like home — an immeasurable wealth in itself, however humble it may be.

CHAPTER 22

OCTOBER MARCHED in becoming a soft tapestry of all the colours of firelight tinting the countryside. Down on to the cottage came the orange tinted leaves, clogging the gutters, while twigs dropped littering the garden, and I would have to sweep them up. In the mornings the garden paths were littered anew. The leaves seemed all on fire and impatient, like miniature flames, which crackled with laughter in the red fire-pits of the logs and peats. Once again the rake and the besom were needed.

In the late afternoons, before shadows gathered round, it was my joy to help Alick Smith, one of the estate workers, to round up the ponies. I usually rode Bess, a chestnut about fifteen hands high. Alick would help me to mount by putting my left foot into the palm of his hands which were clasped.

He would then heave me up onto a glossy coat of velvet. I needed no saddle or bridle, gripping with my knees, I bounced triumphantly to the rhythm of the pony's trot across the park and herded them together, my long light auburn hair, in which Auntie took such pride, blended with the colt's mane. Alick would open wide the gate and digging my heels into her flanks, I shot forward in a powerful leap, throwing a shower of stones skywards. Riding furiously, the road echoed to the clatter of horses' hooves as they followed suit. "That's the rider for you", shouted Alick. in encouragement while, in the frame of the doorway, stood Auntie Barbara at her wits end for fear I would fall off. "Come off that horse at once, you limmer!" she cried, but the sound of galloping hooves drowned her words and I was gone like the wind. Turning in at Farr Lodge gates, I galloped up the back road for about half a mile, then, slowing down, dismounted. The horses' breath were making plumes of mist, going straight up into the air looking like a forest of ghostly fir trees. I gave the mare a kindly pat, and she trotted off, leading the way, to the cattle shed. The scene added a welcome colour to the pale sunlight of the late autumn afternoon. Returning home, I sat and watched the light dying from the sky outside. There in the gloaming, the firelight had a chance to play around the room and weave its quick shadows on the walls.

CHAPTER 23

AS I view the last years of my young days in Strathnairn, happy and memorable days, which belong to the past, never to return, remembering how I was privileged to be a member of that house, and to share the peaceful harmony that reigned within. Its walls standing proudly in the sunlight and solitary amidst the snow in winter. There were times when the moon would ride out across the sky, shedding its brightness on the stone, turning it into a fairy enchanted cottage; and hazy afternoons, the air filled with the myriad sounds of summer with the rustle of wind-stirred leaves and the wild daffodils whipped into a carefree dance. Again, I hear the clarion call of the cock perched on the garden gate, hens cackling as they laid their eggs and somewhere is that faithful friend of man, the sheep dog, barking and the rattle of a milk pail, which brings to my memory one of the many picturesque scenes which hung on the kitchen wall: A gentleman is riding his noble white steed and a milkmaid going a-milking with her pail in her hand. Underneath was written, "Where are you going to my pretty maid? I'm going a milking, sir she said. What is your fortune my pretty maid? My face is my fortune sir she said. Then I'll not marry you my pretty maid. Nobody asked you sir she said." Gazing at this, I pictured myself in a romantic setting, a garden with an orchestra playing softly in the background, blossoms cascading from the trees and myself standing on a balcony gloriously wedded. But, sad to say, there I was left on the shelf like a missing piece of a jig-saw puzzle. I guess they couldn't see me for dust.

Often in an evening I would pay a visit to Maggie Mac-Pherson, who lived with her Auntie, old Mary MacPherson, in a thatched cottage on the edge of a wood, some distance off the beaten track. I remember Maggie telling me that she was born on the stroke of twelve o'clock, and gifted with second sight. She claimed the power of foreseeing events. Sitting on the floor, cross-legged, at her feet, listening to the soft lilt of her Highland accent as she unfolded story after story, I felt I was chained to something deep down and I could not get myself free. It was usually stories of some supernatural experience she had witnessed. Knocks, falling pictures, the shooting star of the night which foretold deaths, or phantom funerals she met at certain points of the road. Journeying home one night she saw one between Farr School and the Free Church — the ghostly horse-drawn hearse with its ghostly driver and sheeted spectres of the populous graveyard moving in mournful procession. Shivers ran up and down my spine and the very hairs of my head seemed to stand on end as the gruesome tale unfolded. They scared me considerably, but I always went back for more. The same place has also been the scene of a battle waged long ago. On the first of May, according to an old legend, people on their way to work had witnessed a skirmish raging in the sky. There were fiery chariots and mounted cavalry fitted with armour of mail, heavy helmets with curving horns and a central crest of a rampant charging boar. They were girt with two handled swords drawn from scabbard between the heavens and the earth grappling with the enemy, their flashing blades spoke with tongues of fire.

Writing about the phantom funeral, my memory flashed back to when I was present at a funeral in the private cemetery in the forest quite near Farr House, once the ancestral home of a branch of the Clan MacKintosh, the last of an ancient family who spent their remaining days in Nairn, fifteen miles from Inverness. I have a faint recollection of hearing the local folk saying that the person's name was Lady Congreve.

The funeral was headed by a Piper, the lament played was "The Flowers of the Forest". I heard the sad, weird notes of the beautiful Pibroch sounding and resounding as the mournful procession wended its way slowly up Farr Avenue, hemmed in on both sides by colourful rhododendrons of breath-catching beauty, surrounded by a wealth of great trees, standing like the companions of Guardian Angels. Over everything hung the strange resplendent canopy of a bright blue sky. The bagpipes lent a majesty, a nobility and a dignity to an important solemn occasion. In the old days, the Piper regularly attended the burial even of the poorest. Before leaving with a funeral it is still not uncommon to serve a round or two of whisky with some breads, biscuits and cheese.

CHAPTER 24

A SHORT distance west the road, nestling on the left-hand side, is "Rose Cottage", sheltered by spruce, pines and fir trees. The stone walls were covered with trellis-work like miniature ladders, with rambling roses cascading from its treads. The lattice windows were full of little diamond shaped leaded panes of glass and the old fashioned porch was made of wood in its natural state, covered with bark. In front was the garden with paths running round both sides of the house. Between the flower beds are stone steps leading down to the little wicker gate, opposite on the other side of the road, two small parks. Round the back a fruit and a vegetable garden, with outhouses and a byre. Below the east side of the house, on point duty, stands a monkey puzzle tree, resembling a giant octopus, and scattered here and there twenty or more bee boxes. Mr and Mrs Rose lived here, with whom I was on excellent terms and frequented their home daily. I was privileged to come and go as I pleased. Auntie Barbara often chaffed me, "You should take your bed there, you only come home here to roost". Mr Rose was a gentleman of excellent breeding and Mrs Rose was tall, elegant and slender, with a sweet voice and a slow smile. She was good and well bred and as worldly wise as she was beautiful. During the summertime the house buzzed with activity. Nephews and nieces were running out and in, shouting and laughing. Rose Cottage was a home of happy scenes—a child's paradise. Mrs Rose had one son, who attended the Royal Academy, Inverness. He stood six feet, topping his father, blue-eyed, a mop of fair curly hair, with a lean handsome face, a good jaw and a firm mouth. He was self-possessed with a fine voice. In my heart there was no-one like Alick Rose. If I saw him coming striding down Rose Cottage brae, I would run and meet him and throw my arms round his waist, laughing up into his face, then I would hang on to his arm and dance by his side. He was steady and serious and loved his books, and was never so happy as when he was planting or weeding in the garden.

My thoughts go back to the many evenings spent in Rose Cottage, seated round the old-fashioned kitchen range, while the older folk would retire to the front parlour. Alick would help me with my lessons, as I often needed help not being quick at my books. He was a wonderful teacher, patient and gentle and made everything so interesting. After lessons were over, he would tease me, singing, "Weel ye gang to the Highlands, Leezie Lindsay" and the other one, "Goodbyee, Don't Sighee". Afterwards we retired to the parlour and would have something hot to drink. At the week-ends, on winter days, Alick would come and ask Auntie Barbara if he could take me sledging. Starting from the top of Rose Cottage brae, Alick steering with his feet and I sitting in the front, we would go whizzing down at terrific speed. At the bottom he insisted that I would stay on, hauling me up the brae. Just before the conclusion of the First World War, Alick was called up along with a number of other lads in the district. Alick joined the Seaforth Highlanders. I remember one cold October evening, I happened to be in Rose Cottage. We were just going to sit down to dinner when Alick blew in, kilt and all, and gathered his beloved mother into his arms, who wept for joy, to have her son back safe and sound. The 1914-18 War was over, brilliantly concluded by the Forces at home and abroad. After a short stay at home, he went to Glasgow University to study for the Medical Profession and where he was capped a Doctor. In my mind's eye I can still picture him, when home on one of his vacations, with his sleeves rolled up and drawing water from the pump at the end of the house, always merry and bright, singing or whistling some Highland air or calling Flossie home to the byre. Oft I stood beside him as he sat on his three-legged stool while he milked the cow, then he would fill a glass with milk and make me drink it. I recall one of the many evenings I spent at Rose Cottage with the lattice windows thrown open wide and one of Alick's sisters playing the piano while he was outside with the violin, and the young folk would dance to a Minuet flitting like butterflies across the lawn in and out of the flower beds and soft strands of music floating across the western pathways of the skies aglow with a lengthening blaze of opalescent fire, made it truly an enchanted evening.

CHAPTER 25

FROM WEST the country came the tinkers' carts, traps and caravans, lumbering leisurely along a procession of men and women of all ages. They had hit the trail sometime in April to reap their harvest bringing with them linen, coloured calico and a glitter of household wares. They were skilled in the art of soldering kettles, pots and pans, in return for a few coppers or some rags and rabbit skins. The tinker tribe were made up of several well-known families.

Old Angus brought his family and their children and his aged mother, who was very much weather-beaten, wrinkled and furrowed about the features and who dearly loved to smoke her little clay pipe. Those tribal folk were not beggars, but rather relics of the ancient clans, forced to take the highway like rolling stones seeking moss: the women folk with their bundles of humanity wrapped in tartan plaids, strapped safely to their backs, and a basket of wares over their arms. They often camped for the night a little way up the back road within sight of the house. Kneeling by the bedroom window, my face pressed against the pane, I watched them, for indeed it was fascinating to see them all squatting round the camp fire, jesting among themselves with steaming mugs of tea in their hands. Later on the women folk would gather their little ones close and retire to the shelter of the caravans. Their horses rested neath the shade of the trees, whose trunks rose up like mighty pillars of an ancient Abbey. While they slept, the camp fire flung back the Autumn darkness, glowing more readily as the wind rose and swept the leaves from the trees. Passing high above the fire, they regained colour for an instant, russet, crimson and gold, looking like a spray from a sea of fire. There were others less fortunate, who travelled later in the year. Encumbered with burdens, their backs bowed, struggling under the weight, they were footsore and weary, their infants cradled to their breast. Like the birds, they too were driven by the storm to the door. My heart went out to the little ones with their grey, starved, pinched faces and wistful eyes. Auntie Barbara would usher them into the house as if she were expecting them and seat them round the glowing hearth and attend to their needs. "Never turn anyone away from the door" she repeated to me many a time and "Never shut the door until they are well away". I remember another one of her sayings, "If anyone came in, never ask them if they would like a cup of tea, prepare it and set it down to them". Their words of thanks were few, but Auntie was well paid by the gratitude expressed in their eyes, as they bid her "good-day". It was nothing unusual to come home from school and find a beggar sitting down to a bowl of broth or a cup of tea.

CHAPTER 26

NOVEMBER BLEW in, unchecked, with the rustle of leaves and the crack of giant boughs heralding the approaching winter. The whistling wind buffeting the windows and screaming round the house echoed dismally. How I loved to dance underneath the trees, to catch the last spinning leaves whose branches in summer united over my head forming an archway of green foliage. But now the Autumn world is dead. The threads of mercury go on falling daily—once more Jack Frost comes out, the window panes become a picture of ferns and flowers. I remember how I used to trace my finger round the pattern, then breathe, making a hole in the frost and stare absorbed into a crystal world, an iron frost held the country-side in its rigid grasp. Hedges and shrubs, rhones and window ledges hung here and there with clusters of icicles like glistening chandeliers. Once again, up in the dark, scrambling through breakfast by candle-light like "Fanny by gas-light" its shadows moved restlessly on the ceiling. Well-clad and gaiters buttoned up to my knees and my gloved hands stuffed in my pocket, I was whirled away to school, the wind bringing with it a flurry of snowflakes spinning and scattering and brushing my cheeks. I called to the others, "Wait for me, wait for me". At times, I nearly got picked up and slung back along the road by the tearing rush of wind. I would bend almost double and force my way step by step. Once more Strathnairn assumes the ghostly appearance of another such winter. Cock Robin would find his way into the house, keeping a wary eye on the drowsy cats. Often he perched on the tip of my finger and fed from my hand and followed me about the house. The Winter has its advantages for with it came the winter sports. Farr Loch would be frozen. Big folk and wee folk, including myself, running and sliding on the ice, while some had skates. I remember two of the party, each taking a hand, whirled me round. Screaming with delight, I found myself gliding like a bird. Suddenly they let me go and I went helter-skelter for a few yards. The next moment I was spread-eagled on the ice. Almost simultaneously I became a target. The battle of the snow started, each making and throwing as fast as they could. Next came sledging. The sledges were made of rudely built frames of common wood with low shod steel runners pro-jecting a few inches in front. Sometimes three of us mounted a sledge at once, depending on the size and following the best and steepest course, we steered with our feet. Too sharp a turning to avoid a clump of bushes, resulted in a confusion of heaped bodies with arms and legs waving frantically in the frosty air, snowlike petals cascading over us. Thus, it would go on till late, under a deep blue night of stars and the loch looking ghostly by moonlight amidst roars of laughter and shrieks of delight. We finished up making a snowman, sticking an old cocked hat on his head and the pipe of peace in his mouth.

At this time of the year there was always a good deal of shooting in the forest, of deer, rabbits and hares. The Game-keeper or the estate workers would go round with a cart depositing a hunk of venison, and game, on every door-step. In the evenings we had a pot of stewed venison, which was very savoury and potatoes crackling with laughter, a jam roly-poly, boiled in a cloth, and the old black iron kettle rumbling by the side of the glowing log and peat fire. How I looked forward to Auntie Barbara's roly-poly, rolled up with home-made jam inside. I always had a second helping. But the supper never tasted so good as when someone dropped in unexpectedly to share in the feast. It somehow tasted better.

CHAPTER 27

DECEMBER COMES round, which has many of the same signs of other Decembers. Sometimes the snow lay so deep that we could not see out of the ground floor window. Always a few weeks before the Festive Season I felt excited and would start to decorate the house, thinking it brought it nearer. I'm afraid I'd never heard of Christmas or Santa Claus till I came to Strathnairn. I recall one of those many Christmases. There were several inches of snow on the ground. I was in my seventh heaven when Auntie and I went to the wood, some-where near Farr House to gather holly, with its never-changing leaves and berries glittering in the mild sun. On Christmas Eve, I hung up my stocking beside the hearth, shaking my head at the thought of Santa's descent. He would surely blacken himself that night! I begged Auntie to leave the door unlocked just in case old Santa changed his mind about the chimney. Watching her face, I saw she smiled quietly to herself as she climbed the stairs with a lighted candle in her hand.

Believe me I could scarcely sleep for excitement—would it never be morning! All of a sudden it was! I jumped up in my nightgown, almost tripping over myself, going downstairs, calling "Merry Christmas". My stocking was stuffed with fascinating knick-knacks. There were transfers, comics, paper hats and a trumpet. I danced about heralding in Christmas. Auntie, about deafened with the noise, chased me off upstairs. Surrounded by my entrancing litter, I sat up in bed enraptured and one by one examined all my trinkets. I was away in a world of my own, rather like "Alice in Wonderland".

New Years of yesterday were occasions for good cheer. We visited each other, passing from home to cottage and from cottage to farm, not forgetting the but-an-ben, drinking each other's health and on New Year's night many of us guests of so-and-so. As I look back on that crowded room, there was much warmth and hand-shaking. There was happiness on their glowing faces, feasting and music, and explosions of laughter, as they were jerked from their seats by the lads to the rhythm of an old-fashioned waltz or a Highland Reel, I recall Auntie Barbara teaching a few of us youngsters the Polka, "first to the heel, then to the toe, that's the way the Polka goes". As midnight approached, the throng would slow down and the toast of the New Year was drunk and all joined hands singing "Auld Lang Syne". Then there was the putting on of coats, wraps and mufflers. As soon as the door was opened the cold air swept in like an invading force and the lights from the lamps flickered in the insistent draught. With "Goodnights" and handshakes, they tumbled out into the starry beauty of the night, tripping over borders and flower beds, to greet other revellers. The trees glittered with frost and like a bubble in the sky, the pale face of the moon peered through a silvery haze.

That old joy and hilarity of the scenes of my childhood, belong to the past. So ended the seven happiest, most carefree years of my life in Strathnairn.

CHAPTER 28

YEAR FOLLOWS year. The festive seasons pass. After the winter darkness come thoughts of springtime. But, alas, like a warning beacon came the appalling news that I was no longer to be supported by the Edinburgh Parish Council and I would have to face the wide world and earn my living, but the very thought of having to leave this vale of memories and the haven which sheltered me for the past seven years was like a knife in my back. For indeed, I was little more than a child and not a very bright child at that. I was far from being equipped for such a journey.

So at fourteen years of age, I started on the next stage of my life. To me it seemed a tragedy, drifting helplessly along to my ironic fate. I was like a ship pounded by a gale. I have an Inverness grocer to thank for my first situation. Through Auntie Barbara he spoke on my behalf to his neighbour who, at that time, was in need of a young girl to help in the house. The night before my departure was one to be remembered. There was much preparing and packing of clothes and my Bible, rolled up in a handkerchief, was put in the corner of my trunk. Then I chased around saying goodbye to neighbours and friends.

Auntie Barbara lectured me on things not done by self-respecting girls, but, I'm afraid, not being adult, I still had my blinkers on and felt a little at sea. I knew nothing of human nature, also, if any doubtful topic of talk cropped up I was to curb my tongue and remain silent. I guess Auntie Barbara's advice was full of good common sense. It was a comforting thought to know that I would always find sanctuary at Eastern Cottage as long as Auntie lived. By this time, the mail car from Whitebridge, driven by Duncan Cameron, Lake View, Stratherrick, replaced the pony trap. So in 1923, on a May morning, the dawn was pale, the air damp and cold, on such a day at a quarter past nine, found Auntie and I, with my little wooden trunk, standing by the roadside, anxiously listening and scanning the highway for a glimpse of the mail car, rattling on its way with its mixed load of humanity, which was to convey us to Inverness. There we spent the greater part of the day visiting Auntie's relatives. In the late afternoon, we hired a horse-drawn cab and proceeded on our way to 15 Kingston, Drummond Road, about a mile out of the town. On my arrival, we were ushered into the diningroom by Mrs Taylor, who has long since passed on. She promised Auntie Barbara she would do everything to make me happy and would teach me all the household duties. She fixed my wages at five shillings per week. While they continued with their arrangements, I stared appraisingly at the furniture. Then we peeped into the kitchen, where our entrance was heralded by a South African parrot, peering through the bars of his gilded cage and shouting, "Hullo there! What do you want? Eh, poor Polly wants a cup of tea, Polly got no dinner today. Poor Polly! Scratch Polly's topie, eh", Panic gripped me. I thought it was the devil himself let loose, for I had never heard of a bird speaking. Mrs Taylor assured me there was no need to be alarmed and introduced me to Polly, who eyed me with keen interest and cackled like an old witch. Promising to write, Auntie took her leave and presently my little wooden trunk was deposited in my bedroom, just off the scullery. From that moment everything ceased to be Paradise. Thus, it was, I became the little maid of all work. My Mistress's mother, Granny Duncan lived here and she was in her ninetieth year and was nearly six feet in height with a back like a ram-rod and was a descendant of the guardians of the soil and mighty proud of it. She was an expert at knitting and whistling. This twelve-roomed house was like a museum. Its walls were decorated with paintings and relics of the South African jungle. The beautiful inlaid oak floors were carpeted with leopard and lion skins and Persian rugs and it was indeed a well kept establishment. My Mistress was a very methodical person and had every minute of the day planned beforehand. I needed no alarm-clock to wake me in the mornings. Old Polly performed that beautifully whistling "Up in the morning early" with every note as true and clear as a bell. He gave me no peace till I rose and took his cover off. It was like a sieve full of holes. For weeks I was homesick. On saying my prayers at bed-time, I was often seized by a swift flow of tears, a relapse into baby-hood, a sense of loss and desolation overwhelmed me. The mornings found me dressed in a white cap and apron, brandishing a broom. I could understand wearing an apron, but not the cap and concluded it was to keep my hairs from falling into the soup. Believe me, without exaggeration, my Mistress had a problem on her hands. She had taken on no easy task. I was backward and awkward, even in sweeping the floor. I swept the centre and shoved the dust into a corner or under the carpet. My Mistress was often blamelessly exasperated and almost at the end of her tether, sending me back so often to do it all over again. You can imagine what Auntie Barbara was like and she must have sometimes been at the end of her tether. She once remarked to me, "I'm sorry for the man who takes you for a wife". My Mistress did a good deal of the work herself, including the cooking. But soon I was bustling around handling crockery, kettles and frying pans all at once. There were days when Polly screeched all day long and even swore at me. Many times he told me to "go to hell out of here" and time and again I threatened him with the broom, but forty year old Polly defied me. Sometimes my Mistress left me in charge of the lunch while she went out shopping in the town. You may be sure I peeped into every pot and casserole dish and poked my little finger in to taste it. Polly never missed anything and I would be reminded, "Polly wants a bittie too eh", "Poor Polly". "Lizzie's boy eh". Just before my Mistress was due home for lunch I scooted out to the garden swing and swung with the greatest of ease. The maid next door, hanging out her washing one day, looked over the garden wall and thought I had gone crazy and laughed till her sides ached. It was no laughing matter when I heard her ladyship's footsteps on the gravel. I went shooting through the air, jumped off and darted indoors, taking a quick look at the lunch simmering. I then bustled off to finish my dusting, doing it the quickest way possible, by blowing it. Had there been a bellows handy I would have made good use of it. If I broke anything my Mistress never fussed. "Nothing lasts forever" she would say cheerfully, "Wipe up the mess, child, but first wipe your eyes". Left alone with the broken dish I sat on the floor and tried to piece it together. When cleaning upstairs I sometimes found myself gazing out of the window. My eyes travelled over the roofs and belching chimney pots, dreaming, if only I had a Fairy Godmother like Cinderella. Probably I would have asked her to find my papa and mother. I would return to earth with the door-bell ringing in my ears. I slid down the banisters when the Mistress wasn't there, the quickest way I thought. The first time, I landed in a heap at the bottom. However, practise made me perfect. Often the door-bell rang when I was in the middle of dish-washing and scouring pans. Drying my hands on my apron, and adjusting my cap, I would go skidding through the hall and with a Cheshire grin on my face, peacocked the caller into the drawing room. I made a terrible mess of myself when cleaning the gas cooker and the anthracite stove. My face especially became smudged all over. In the state I was in, I was asked if I had been up the chimney. By the afternoons, I was the last dirty piece to clean up. Tea was at four-thirty and found me with my leg cocked up, panting and manoeuvreing a large tray on my knee and nearly dropping it in an effort to manage the sitting room door handle. The evenings were engaged in ironing and cleaning silver with old Polly as my sole companion. Occasionally, on a Saturday or Sunday evening, my Mistress's two nephews, Joseph and Donald, called in, two sturdy, kilted laddies, who lived a little way up Drummond Road. They always invaded my quarters first, shouting, "Hallo fuzzie Lizzie, busy Lizzie" and then the fun started. They were in their element when I chased them with the broom-stick and they would make a beeline for the bathroom upstairs, turning the tap full on and squirted the water with their fingers, baptising me unconditionally as I rushed in after them. On hearing the rumpus, old Granny Duncan would ascend the stairs to read out the riot act, shouting and waving her stick in the air she sounded rather like old Polly raging.

Before the boys departed, I had a ride on one of their bicycles, forgetting I was supposed to be grown up with my hair in a bun at the back of my head, and hair pins, like miniature pitch-forks keeping it in place. Putting my leg over the cross-bar I streaked away down Drummond Road, my white apron strings flapping in the air and my cap lying somewhere on the highway, while Joseph and Donald looked on, roaring with laughter and shouting, "there goes Granny on her scooter". To dismount, I had to manoeuvre up against a lamp-post as, hampered by my long clothes, I could not swing my leg over the bar. They, too, have passed on.

The months flashed by, and I began to feel run down and grew listless. Old Doctor England Kerr visited me from time to time. I was troubled with my back. My Mistress was extremely kind and with her past nursing experience, massaged me every night before going to bed. I longed for home and Auntie Barbara, which would have been more than the prescription required. As I began to expand, my cottons and flannels began to shrink. My stays, with the shoulder strap were becoming more difficult to fasten and the buttons of my petticoats would not meet at the back. However, waist strings and neck strings could still tie and hold all in its place. I became sizeable to my Mistress's cast-offs. They were lovely long combinations, reaching nearly below the calf of the leg. I tucked the frills and laces inside my hand-knitted hose while my black elastic garters below the knee, kept them in place. The gowns reached nearly to my ankle base. I felt so proud wearing them to thread bare end. Beggars can't be choosers. I always remember when, wishing for anything new, Auntie Barbara quoting me, "If wishes were horses then beggars would ride". My Mistress banked my money. When I had sufficient amount saved, the first thing I bought was a pair of cloth boots for Auntie Barbara, which only cost twelve shillings and sixpence. I begun to grow restless and longed for a change. I had been here over two years, so in the month of May, I preened my slender wings for flight. Back home to the old folks. Once more I roamed in the haunts of the deer by loch and stream.

CHAPTER 29

DURING MY stay at home, I was introduced to a Mrs MacKintosh, a friend of Auntie Barbara's sister-in-law who was cook-housekeeper to Mr and Mrs Sedgewick from London and came north every year for the fishing season, also the shooting season on their estate, Farraline House, Stratherrick. So, on the 7th August, 1925, I joined the staff in the twenty-roomed house as scullery maid. My monthly wage was two pounds, ten shillings. As the youngest member I was never spoilt so beautifully and was given a great deal of freedom.

The little scullery off the kitchen, with its wee iron sink, just held myself and the pots. Beyond the window stood the plucking shed, and down below the burn gurgled through a channel fringed with mosses and ferns. Alongside the scullery was the pantry window where Dan MacKay, the Postman, stood many a day courting the fair-haired Gwendoline, the second table-maid. I spent the forenoons skinning rabbits, hares and all kinds of game. Some of the game was so very "high" and could only be used for the stock-pot. It was one of my many joys when Mrs MacKintosh or Mary, the kitchen maid, left a scraping of something in the pans. It somehow tasted better. The food here was excellent. By a quarter past two I was free and, if not too tired, I got old Rory, the Ghillie, to saddle Gip for me and took a canter round the grounds. Mrs Sedgewick was often in her boudoir window to greet me with a wave as I passed. I was never happier than when I was in the saddle. I usually went on duty about a quarter past seven. I had the vegetables to cook for the diningroom and the staff. This was my little bit of responsibility. I recall at bed-time tormenting Mary, the kitchen maid and Annie, the house-maid, with whom I shared a bedroom, somersaulting all over the beds. When they couldn't find their night attire, they took an end each and bumped me up and down on the floor. I recall one night producing a feather which I pulled from the tail of a cock-pheasant in the plucking shed. Amidst the squeaking of bed springs, I crept out over to the girls and tickled their noses. To me, this was great fun, but it was more than they could stand. They gave vent to a most unearthly shriek, giving me a bigger fright. I darted back to bed, covered myself up and broke into a fit of infectious giggles. There was a scuffle of feet outside the door and in popped the head house-maid, "Is that you, Lizzie, making all that noise?" she enquired. "When ever will you grow up?" Laughing, I apologised. She smiled and came over and tucked me in, saying, "there's a good girl, now go to sleep".

About the middle of October I journeyed south with the staff to their London residence, 29 Norfolk Street, Park Lane, London, S.W.1. Here we were left in charge and given board wages, as Mr & Mrs H. B. Sedgewick spent the winter months in their country house at Hook Heath Farm, Woking, Surrey. This was my first visit to London. For a while I was not allowed to go out alone. Mrs Mackintosh or some of the staff acted as chaperon. On Armistice Day I got my first view of the Royal Family, as King George V laid a wreath at the foot of the Cenotaph. Every Sunday Mrs Mackintosh took me to the Presbyterian Church. Even during the week my religious devotions were not neglected. I was taken on Wednesday to an evening prayer meeting, held in Eccleston Hall near Victoria Station. Here I met many Scots and began to feel a link with my old country. Life ebbed and flowed tranquilly.

My first impression of London was one of confused bewilderment. It was not like anything I had ever seen. London, the Capital of the British Empire — this unique city, its age, its traditions and its extraordinary dignity of picturesque beauty and splendour. I observed thronging crowds of all nations, of all ranks, of all conditions, the handsome triple gateway, leading to the fashionable part of Hyde Park, facing Park Lane — the home of millionaires. Like Grosvener Square it is the lap of luxury. Since then both have suffered from new poverty and flats have replaced lordly mansions. Beyond Hyde Park lie Kensington Gardens, full of beautiful flowers. A favourite spot with children is the fanciful statue of Peter Pan, the boy who never grew up. It stands on the west bank of Long Water where, in Sir James Barrie's play, he is supposed to have roamed. There was Fleet Street, the traditional headquarters of journalism, though many newspapers have flitted elsewhere. Piccadilly Circus, the centre of traffic and pleasure, in the West End, with advertisements and neon signs everywhere. High above the city soars the magnificent Cathedral of St. Paul's. The dome, a very imposing feature, stands out as one of the most striking landmarks in the world. It is with pleasure I remember the tameness of the pigeons, with absolutely no fear of human beings, one of London's greatest attractions. I recall evenings spent wandering along the Thames embankment and watching the straggling rows of lights on either side of the river. Standing on Westminster Bridge, I heard the sonorous chimes of Big Ben, vibrating through the city. Now and then a small boat drifted past with a lantern in its stern. The noise of London was a subdued hum behind me as I watched old Father Thames rolling along to empty himself in the basin of the ocean. Amidst all this picturesque beauty and splendour of the old and the new, harmonising in this ancient unique city, I felt lost and my heart yearned for the heather clad hills of home. One day I was sitting in Hyde Park, when a dolled-up slip of a girl sat down beside me. Suddenly a smart car came to a standstill beside the kerb. The girl on the seat fluttered her eyelashes. A code message had just been flashed, and the driver flicked open the door of his jollopy and off they shot. Presently an old duffer with a top hat and a swallow tail coat made a bold pass at me, and pretended that he knew me. He called me his darling and said he hadn't seen me for a long time. He even took my arm and tried to pilot me away. I was terrified. I told him he was an old fool on the brink of eternity and rather reluctantly he sailed off in search of other prey.

During the early spring of 1927, Mr H. B. Sedgewick sent a firm of electrical engineers north to Farraline House, where a shelter was erected beside the burn, opposite the plucking shed, and an electric plant installed thus doing away with the paraffin lamps. I was glad when the month of May came round and we returned to Scotland. The winds were still cold, but there was a healthy tang of the brown old earth everywhere and a few patches of snow in the folded hollows of the hills. The fishing season on Farraline Estate lasted three weeks, then we were given a cheque for more than two months wages, with fifteen shillings per week board wages, until our return on the 7th August, in time for the "Glorious Twelfth". Mr H. B. Sedgewick was Chief Director of Lloyds Bank in London.

On the 13th March 1928, before our return to Scotland, I was fortunate to catch a glimpse of King Amanullah and Queen Seryia of Afghanistan on their state visit to King George and Queen Mary. They were met at Dover by the Prince of Wales and at Victoria Station by their Majesties and received as guests at Buckingham Palace. If I remember correctly the newspaper described King Amanullah as being five feet tall and every inch a King.

During the shooting season of 1928, my health broke down and I came home once again to my Auntie's cottage in Strathnairn.

CHAPTER 30

THERE IS beauty in Strathnairn, whatever the season. As the snows vanish the days lengthen, snowdrops and crocuses with their escort of golden daffodils fill the air with fragrance. It was one of those days in the month of April 1929, I was busy delving and transplanting in the garden, when the present Mrs MacKenzie of Farr called to enquire if I could be spared to help in Farr House. "I'm very sorry, Mrs MacKenzie" Auntie Barbara said, "but Lizzie is engaged to go to Achnacarry Castle at the beginning of May for the fishing season." "Oh! She's going to Lochiel's! How nice!" I had seen the post advertised in the local newspaper and had promptly applied and got the job. So, as much as I would have liked to have stayed in the Strath, I was destined to venture further afield, this time into Lochaber.

Achnacarry Castle, standing erect like a monarch lording over the glen, has long been the home of the Cameron Chiefs beautifully situated amidst a sweeping panorama of magnificent grandeur. In summer that wild beauty reveals itself cradled in a wealth of greenery like a picture stepping out of a geography book. Near the site stands vestiges of a castle burnt by the Duke of Cumberland, 1746. According to history it was on the Gairlochy Road, leading to Spean Bridge, seven miles away, at the time of the '45, that Lochiel, riding his charger, was approached by an old woman, who emerged from behind some trees and addressed him, "Lochiel, Lochiel, beware of the day when the Lowlands shall swipe thee in battle array." The brave Lochiel could not foresee the danger, and history relates, he was involved in the defeat of the Prince. For himself, he won the title of "The Gentle Lochiel" because of his mildness and goodness and his love of peace. Achnacarry Castle is but a shadow of its original self. Once the scene of bygone glory, time can only add new lustre to the memory of the past. When speaking to Lochiel, we addressed him as "Lochiel" and Lady Hermione, "Your

Ladyship". The fishing season there lasted three months and during this period, Lochiel entertained many famous guests, notably the Duke of Gloucester. Naturally, I was confined to the kitchen quarters and kept busy cleaning fish and skinning eels, nasty slippery creatures, which even wriggled when they were dead. My wages were three pounds per month, with laundry and insurance stamps. I also cooked the vegetables and dished them up for the dining room and staff. Lochiel's piper, Norman MacRae, a picturesque Highlander was also butler and valet and ever faithful to his trust, preserved the customs and ideas of a former age. Early in the morning the household woke to the skirl of the pipes from the Castle grounds with Pibrochs and the familiar notes of "The March of the Cameron Men" keeping up an old Highland tradition. Every night, just before dinner, the dining room resounded to the skirl of the Pibroch, amidst a brilliant display of white damask, crystal and flashing silver. In the staff hall he was always the life of the party, with his happy sense of humour.

The road from Clunes on Loch Lochy to the foot of Loch Arkaig, is locally known as "the dark mile" due to the prevalence of gigantic trees which interweave their branches and blot out the sunlight. I remember one afternoon speeding along "the dark mile" on a borrowed bicycle when the wheel caught in a rut and I was thrown on to the road, injuring my left leg. I crippled back to the Castle and made my way through the glass court, where I bumped into Mrs MacRae, the piper's wife, who was house-keeper and Lady's maid. She was greatly concerned about my dishevelled appearance and took me into her sewing room, where she bathed my wounds. I still carry the scar on my leg — a souvenir of the "dark mile".

The fishing season ended, and I travelled as far as Inverness with the staff, who were journeying on to Lochiel's summer residence in Nairn, but here we parted company and I made tracks for home and Auntie Barbara.

After a month at home, I went to Moy Hall, the seat of the

Mackintosh of Mackintosh, situated on the Northern bank of Loch Moy. It was here in February 1746 that Prince Charles Edward Stuart arrived as a guest of Lady Mackintosh. Only a few servants and retainers were within call. Lord Louden, in charge of the Hanoverian troops in Inverness, planned the capture of the Prince, the knowledge of the plot leaked out and a boy and a girl were sent out by different routes to warn the Prince and only just succeeded in reaching Moy Hall in time. Lady Mackintosh, in the absence of her husband, had few men to defend Moy Hall. Donald Fraser, the steward and blacksmith, on being warned of the danger, armed his six trusty men, ever courageous and daring, ready to do-or-die when the fate of their Prince and Country rested on the point of their swords. Donald Fraser, by putting his ear close to the turf, heard the trampling of feet which heralded the approach of Lord Louden's forces. He dispersed his followers throughout the woods. Then, at a given signal, the hidden men fired their muskets as quickly as possible and almost simultaneously with their bagpipes, raised the slogan of their various clans. The Hanoverians were completely hoaxed. Thinking that the Jacobite army was upon them, they took to their heels and fled. Only one shot was fired and by a strange fate, it killed the famous MacLeod piper, Mac-Crimmon who, before leaving his home, had composed that beloved piece of Pipe music, "MacCrimmon's Lament", This incident in history has been handed down through the years and recorded as the "Rout of Moy".

Six weeks at Moy for me were spent cleaning copper pots and frying pans of every sort and size. Many were heavy and clumsy and took all my strength to lift them. It was a full day's work keeping them clean. This I did by using silver sand and vinegar, rinsed off with a lather of soft soap and dried quickly. They shone like a new penny straight from the mint. It was a pleasant surprise, one afternoon, to greet the arrival of Lochiel's piper, Norman MacRae and his wife. Lochiel and Lady Hermione had come as guests to Moy Hall and as was their custom, were accompanied by their personal staff. At the end of my six weeks stay, Cook presented me with a small red, white and blue posy, she had bought at a Sale-of-Work. It had been made by the little hands of a little lassie, the grand-daughter of the Mackintosh chief. I've always kept it as a remembrance of my stay in Moy Hall.

My next move was to Farr House, home of Major and Mrs MacKenzie, where over the Christmas period, I was asked to give the housemaids a helping hand. Major Alexander MacKenzie, JP was Commissioner to King George V and every year, the family journeyed to Ard-Na-Coille on Balmoral Estate, when the Royal Family were in residence at Balmoral Castle. How I enjoyed hearing little scraps of news about the Royal Family from the staff on their return home to Farr House.

Calling on the Major one day, the King was met at the door by the Major's youngest son, Master Sandy. "Well, little black face, is your father in?" asked the King. Master Sandy was never so happy as when he was playing games with the local boys especially football regardless of mud and dripping clothes. And for a time the nick-name stuck — "Little black-face".

CHAPTER 31

APRIL 1930 saw me employed as house table-maid in the home of Doctor James Murray, 6 Ardross Terrace, Inverness, a very eccentric old gentleman who hailed from the Bonnie Black Isle. He was over eighty years of age. His wife claimed she was a descendant of Sir Walter Scott. During the autumn she became so critically ill that she really required the services of a trained nurse. But her husband, who attended her, would not hear of such a thing and I was assigned to all duties at her bedside. She was full of the childish complaints of old age and as unpredictable as the ocean winds. As she grew a little better and was able to sit up, I had to sit with her during the evenings reading endlessly aloud. Gradually she demanded my presence more and more. At bed-time I vacated her room as soon as possible, leaving her supping her beverage. Tired, after a long day's work, I began to feel the effect of fatigue. Many a time I went to bed faint with tiredness and sinking wearily down on the bed, sobbed myself to sleep. Little did Doctor Murray guess how the strain was affecting me, but when his wife recovered sufficiently to regain her feet, he could not thank me enough for what I had done. His gratitude was recompense indeed. However, fatigue had left its mark and shortly afterwards I became ill suffering from nervous debility. Doctor Ian MacLeod advised me to give up my duties in Doctor Murray's house and so I returned home, to Auntie Barbara. What would I have done without her?

CHAPTER 32

WINTER PASSED, Strathnairn wakened once more to the hope and promise of another Spring. By this time I regained my strength, so on the 1st April 1931, I set forth to the house of Sir William Coats Cross, Bart, Scatwell House, Scatwell, Ross-shire, as second table-maid. Here I improved my education in domestic work tutored by the head parlour-maid, Katie Ann, soon becoming adept at cleaning the silver every day before use and laying the dining room table. I also learned to wait at the table. The crystal and glassware were priceless valuables and the fruit plates, knives and forks were of solid gold. Katie Ann taught me how to use the private telephone switchboard when sending messages to London for Sir William. I had also to valet for Mr Cowan, Sir William's secretary. During the season I remember the Derby Race in June and we had a sweepstake and I sunk a shilling on the favourite — the "Cameronian" — who with a one-track mind won the Derby Cup, enriching me by one pound, seven shillings and sixpence. One day a Government Official called at Scatwell House, taking a census. I was very much embarrassed when asked to give my full name and address, date and place of birth, I did not know it and Eastern Cottage was the only address of which I was aware. Yet I knew at the time I was an incomer to the Strath and I decided there and then to try and seek information about my parentage. I wrote to the Edinburgh Parish Council who forwarded the address of an Aunt living in the Dean Village and suggested that I should contact her.

This information started me thinking far back in my memory. I had very vague recollections of my childhood, which, in my later happiness in Strathnairn, I had tried to forget. I wrote to this Aunt and by return post I received an invitation to visit her in the Dean Village. Enclosed was a photograph of an Uncle, Sergeant William McKay, Australian Imperial Forces, taken in Piershill Studio. I had come to a turning point in my young life.

I wrote home to Auntie Barbara, explaining and told her not to worry. The urge had come into my heart to discover more about myself and my background. Who was my mother? Why had she deserted me? Was she dead? Also, was my Papa dead? A few days later, before I was due to leave Scatwell House, Sir William's secretary, Mr Cowan, called me into his sittingroom to ask if I would stay on. But I assured him of my other plans and that I intended leaving at the end of the month. I was all keyed up with excitement for my first visit to Edinburgh since I had left there as a child at the age of seven to be boarded out.

CHAPTER 33

ON THE first of July, 1931, I arrived in Edinburgh in the late afternoon, and from the top of Waverley Steps hailed a taxi which drove me to the foot of Queensferry Street.

There I decided to walk the rest of the way down the cobbled brae, past a garage and the Sunday School. My footsteps sounded loud and strange; I almost ran feeling as if I had stepped out into another world. Suddenly I heard the rushing waters of the River Dean. I stood gazing around me for I was in the heart of the Dean Village. Sights, sounds and smells made the past live again, a flood of memories came sweeping over me, everything here reminded me of my nine months in the Dean Village. I had the dimmest memory of my Papa. Walking slowly I recognised the house I had known so well, No. 2 Hawthornbank Buildings. I must confess I approached it with some inward shrinking. I paused at the door, drew a long breath and knocked loudly. Presently light footsteps shuffled within and, as the door slowly opened, the face of my Aunt peered at me in the glow from the lighted candle that she held in her hand. She had a shawl wrapped round her shoulders and her face was pale and thin, set with obstinate lines of habitual grievances, but her smile was oddly gentle. I stood hesitatingly in the doorway. This was our first meeting since that terrible parting in Craiglockhart Workhouse. There was no necessity for introductions and she beckoned me over the threshold. "It's been a long time Lizzie," she murmured softly taking me by the hand, "Yes Auntie," I mumbled, "It's been a long time." "I'll never forget when I took you to the Workhouse, your cries and screams haunted me for many a long day," she whispered, and covered her face with her hands. "Never mind Auntie, it's all over now and I've come back. You know, I am twenty-two years old now." She looked at me, the tears streaming down her face, "How you have grown," her voice was at breaking point, "I never expected to see you like this." We had much to say to each other but I had a feeling that she knew what was uppermost in my mind. At last, I could not hold it back any longer. "Auntie", I said, "please, my Papa, is he dead"? "Yes Lizzie a long time ago, your Papa was very ill. You remember when he came to see you at the weekends", "Yes Auntie, I remember", and how he used to teach me to say my prayers kneeling down by the bedside. I made the sign of the cross, then clasped my hands, "My Mother, is she alive?" I asked. "Yes Lizzie but it would be much better if you had nothing to do with her, she's no good and she never wanted you. When your brother Francis was killed, you were born twelve days later and your mother threatened to take your life if you lived, so Auntie Nellie handed you over to the care of an old couple in Montrose." Her words were severe but the tone was not unkind but I felt an unexpressed sympathy behind the inevitable dryness. One must weigh the good against the evil. Auntie never mentioned the nature of my brothers accident and I did not enquire. Francis was six years nine months when he met his death. Auntie also told me that my Grandfather, Jock MacKay, was a horse dealer in Stockbridge, and Granny MacKay had a small fish shop. She was a Duncan before she married my Grandfather and they hailed from Durness, Sutherland.

My grand-uncles and uncles emigrated to Australia before the first World War and Uncle Willie, whose photo I had been sent, came over with the Australian Imperial Forces during the 1914 War. While stationed in Piershill Barracks he had visited my mother and rebuked her considerably for her neglect of me. He had wanted to take me back with him to Australia but by this time I was out of touch and safely deposited in the heart of the Highlands.

CHAPTER 34

THE NEXT day after my arrival in Edinburgh I pleaded with my Aunt, "Tell me, please, where can I find my mother?" At last she gave in, "All I can tell you Lizzie is that as far as I know she was living under an assumed name of 'Hume' in Portobello and takes in boarders." Auntie gave me no address. I had only a name to work on and I didn't even know what she looked like. I was crusading in pursuit of happiness and was determined to find my mother at all costs. A few days later, without saying a word to Auntie. I boarded a tramcar outside the General Post Office to take me to Portobello. Arriving there I began my investigations. Wearily I trudged from one boarding establishment to another and from house to house asking if they knew of a Mrs Hume who took in boarders. It was a desperate search and all I got was a shake of the head, nobody knew her. Some force stronger than myself seemed to drive me on. The afternoon was far spent and it began to rain heavily; all was drab and dreary. I took shelter in a doorway of a small baker's shop at the foot of Bath Street. I had forgotten to eat and my head ached as I stood listening to the pitter patter of rain on the pavement. It was like going down into the bottom of the sea to look for my mother. I was conscious of a dull sense of misery. I've just got to find my mother I kept repeating to myself. The rain ceased and it suddenly dawned on me that perhaps the girls in the shop might know. Going in I approached one of them and said quite cautiously, "I don't suppose you know of a Mrs Hume who takes in boarders?" She thought for a minute and then said, "Try number thirty Bath Street, just a few doors along on this side, one floor up, there is such a person living there." I thanked her — at that moment I never felt more alive. I ascended the wide spacious stone stairs, my sodden shoes squelching, my breath coming short and hard. I paused at the head of the stairs, I could hear the tumultuous pounding of my heart. I pulled the shiny brass bell. The door opened — instinct told me that I had found my mother as she stood framed in the doorway, her unflinching stare transfixing me till I felt like an eel on the spit. Her features were perfect as if they had been chiselled. She had an excellent figure, full but not stout and her height would be about five feet one. As my mother stood there, her head tilted a little to one side and her mouth parted a little in a smile, I fought desperately for words. Speaking carefully, as if I were feeling my way over a bog, I said, "Perhaps you could help me please, I'm looking for digs?" She kept staring at me. "Come in", she said at last, "You are very wet". On entering the house I suddenly felt afraid. I waited for her to speak. "Where do you come from?" my mother asked. "The Dean Village", I replied softly. She did not speak but just stared and stared at me as if she were seeing a ghost. Slowly she sat down on a sofa. "You are Lizzie", she said. Tears blurred my eyes, "Yes, and you are my mother", I said. My voice faltered, my emotions almost choked me. This was a supreme tremendous moment for me. I had found my mother — the woman who had cast me out, unwanted. There was compassion on her face as her hand slowly reached out towards me. I hovered uncertainly then suddenly broke down with a heart-rent sob. "Mother, Mother!" I cried piteously and burst into a flood of tears as she drew me into the circle of her arms as if I were a tiny child in need of comfort. I was unaware of hunger and fatigue, only of a strange overflowing of happiness that sought relief in weeping. My feelings for my mother were strong so that all other figures in my life became as distant shadowy forms in a dream. To my knowledge, this was the first time my mother had set eyes on me since I was twenty-one days old. She insisted on calling me 'Betty', short for Elizabeth.

Returning to the Dean Village that evening Auntie guessed to where I had disappeared and made no comment. I mentioned that my mother wished me to go and live with her and had promised to make up for the past. "Well Lizzie", she said, a trifle coldly, "Don't say I haven't warned you." The following day I joined my mother. She no longer went under the name of Hume. Evidently she had just been married a year, the second time, to a Mr James Davidson, I understood they were married before the Sheriff. Her husband was more or less an invalid and walked with the aid of crutches as both his legs were amputated below the knees. For some unknown reason she did not wish her husband to know that I was her daughter so I was introduced as a cousin. The days that followed were a taste of paradise. The weeks flashed by. Then about the middle of September my mother closed the house in Portobello and we journeyed up to her flat at twenty-two Buccleuch Street, Edinburgh. During that period Mr Davidson sensed a closer relationship in me than a cousin of the woman he had wed. He broached the subject to my mother one day. Then it all came out and my tale of woe was slowly unfolded. Yet he could not have been kinder to me. But after the disclosure, alas, my mother changed. There were days when I was conscious of a faint discomfort I could not define. Oft-times I detected a cynical gleam in her steely blue eyes. I began to feel I was meanly regarded and was made to feel my dependence. I suspect she saw I wasn't bursting with talent and I began to avoid her and creep out of the way.

One night my mother returned from a Whist Drive, I was busy preparing the supper and I sensed something strange about her. There was a silence as sudden as follows a loud noise and I felt an icy premonition coursing down my spine; a storm was brewing; it came in a way I had not expected. My mother let fly with her hand and struck me leaving me sick and trembling. Her face began to flush dangerously, her eyes smouldering with jealousy. I stared at her unbelievingly. the violence of her emotions stirred in me some pity for her and somehow I could not dislike her. Suddenly she picked up a knife; a chill of terror as I had never known before froze my blood. Mr Davidson stood stricken and bewildered at the sudden turn of events and then shouted frantically, "Run Betty, through to the room." As I stumbled blindly from her presence I heard the knife clatter to the floor, my mother followed and beat me with passionate fury, once lifting her foot she kicked me, that kick flashed back an almost forgotten memory of another such kick I had received long ago. Once again the tragedy that surrounded my birth had overwhelmed her. I was hurled from my sunlit peak of happiness into a world of darkness. Weeping I gathered my bundle together, wrenched the door open and fled from the house and was swallowed up in the darkness. The cold air struck my burning

Miss Elizabeth 'Suzie' McKay at the age of 30.

Farr Public School, Strathnairn, which I attended from the age of seven.

A class photograph at Farr Public School where I am pictured in the middle row, extreme left.

face, it was past midnight and the streets were almost deserted. I made my way to the Dean Village, my head throbbed and swam, the wind sang and sobbed through the streets, the shop signs rattled and screeched to and fro and threw their shadows around me. All was drab and all seemed to be mocking me. Pulling up the collar of my coat, I dragged myself along, my knees almost giving way. On reaching the Dean Village Auntie was not the least surprised to see me as she sat huddled by the fire, in a drunken stupor, the dirty end of a cigarette sagging from her lips. I crouched down beside the dwindling fire, sick and shivering and wept wildly and passionately as I had never wept before. Some pain can be withstood but not the pain and anguish of the heart and before I went to bed there was something I had to know. "Tell me truthfully, Auntie, during the nine months I lived with you, one evening you were preparing to go out, who was the woman standing by. You remember I was crying and she lifted her foot and kicked me. "Who was it Auntie?" She hesitated for a moment and without raising her eyes said, "It was your own mother Lizzie, that was the first time she saw you since you were twenty-one days old." Her words fell heavily like a blow on the head. I staggered from the fireside like a wounded animal longing to be left alone. As I analyse my life's history I have still to come to the most tragic part, which I shall find very difficult to write down.

The moment that I fled from Buccleuch Street I knew myself to be an exile. In spite of what happened I hungered for my mother as she was part of me and I was part of her. Overpoweringly weary, though I was, I had enough sense to realise that I could not stay here and be housed like a beggar. My Aunts attitude towards me was none too pleasant. I suspect she too sensed I wasn't bursting with talent.

I had less than three pounds between myself and the Work-house. The following day I packed my few belongings together and journeyed to Montrose by bus. On looking round I was once again reminded of the past. As I walked slowly down South

Esk Street, the houses huddled together, each speaking out its own history amid the blast of the wind, in my mind's eye I saw an old man and an old woman in the small but-and-ben in this little country town and a lump rose in my throat. I took a walk up to the burial ground and saw the grave where their mortal remains lie. I turned away and proceeded towards the harbour where I, the waterfront child, had often wandered. Dotted here and there were fishing craft, catching the rays of the autumn sunshine turning them into pale gold. On my way back I saw my first school of learning at the age of five, pausing for a moment or two, once again I saw myself a wee lassie, one in a crowd yet all alone. Without knowing it my footsteps led me to the workhouse and gazing at it for a moment, I remembered, as though a knife pierced my flesh. With a sob I almost ran from it. (People can't treat human beings inhumanly without leaving scars on those they ill-use). From Montrose I journeyed by bus to Aberdeen hoping I would have a better chance of finding some kind of work.

This was my first visit to the Granite City by the sea.

CHAPTER 35

WANDERING AROUND in a daze I managed to find a make-shift for the night in a boarding house in George Street. The next day I asked someone to direct me to an Employment Agency. That very day I was given an address.

St Margaret's Convent, 17 Spital, Old Aberdeen, which turned out to be a religious order called Sisters of Charity belonging to the Scottish Episcopal Church of Scotland. As I reached the gate there was quite a steep brae to climb leading to the two story building joining the Chapel which stood a hundred feet above sea level. There were two front entrances, I went to the one on the right, and picking up courage rang the door bell. There was the sound of a scuffle of feet inside, slowly the door was opened by a very old Sister whom I got to know as Sister Sarah. A feeling of panic gripped me as she beckoned me to follow her along the dimly lit passage to a waiting room which had a polished wooden floor. The silence engulfed me amd I began to wonder what I had let myself in for. In a matter of seconds another Sister came along, a Sister Caroline, who engaged me right away, told me my duties and showed me to my bedroom which turned out to be a cubicle. Thanking her I took my leave and went to fetch my belongings from my make-shift in George Street.

October 1931 I started work. There were other three of a staff, young girls, one kitchen-maid, two house-maids and myself, who had the laying of the tables in the refectory for the Sisters and, as they took in a few guests, I had the bedrooms to keep clean and the guest room to look after, also help Sister Caroline with the older Sisters who were bedridden and the usual bedroom chores.

Once I settled down I signed on to Doctor Rorie's panel. Gradually the past incidents began to fade away and I settled down to my new surroundings. We girls had to take week about of blowing the Chapel organ for the Sisters when they went into vespers at six o'clock. Once I nearly went to sleep working the handle of the organ up and down, when Sister Emily's head bobbed round the corner and whispered as loud as she dared, "Blow, blow," only the voices of the choir Sisters could be heard down in their stalls. This was the first time in my life that I had ever seen a Nun, I regarded them with a feeling of reverential awe. They wore dark grey habits, white hoods and broad white collars. In the mornings it looked comical to see them all donned with large white aprons over their habits, going about their daily chores. They looked all the world like penguins, their long sleeves flapping by their sides as they strutted in and out the dimly lit corridors. One morning I slept in so with my house slippers in my hand, the wooden stairs being highly polished, I slipped and went hurtling down, slippers and all, and landed at the bottom with a bump, the noise woke poor old Sister Sarah; I was still sitting at the bottom of the stairs feeling sorry for myself when Sister opened her bedroom door. I explained what happened and that I was all right, putting my slippers on I made myself scarce to make up for lost time.

While I was there I was introduced to two Welfare Officers, a Miss Russell and a Miss Archibald, from Drumsheugh Gardens, Edinburgh. Little did I know that in due course we were fated to meet under the most painful and tragic circumstances. I wrote home to Auntie Barbara to let her know of my whereabouts since I left Scatwell House at the end of June, 1931.

In the summer of 1934 Auntie was suddenly taken ill, was rushed to the Royal Northern Infirmary, where she successfully underwent an operation for a burst appendicitis, at the age of eighty-five. By the time my fortnight's holiday was due she was out of hospital recuperating in her niece's hotel, Bains Temperance Hotel, Castle Street, Inverness. So early one morning I boarded the train for Inverness and went to see her. She was very comfortable and well looked after. I stayed a few days and then took the bus home to Strathnairn to get the chimneys cleaned and put the house in order. I wrote and asked Sister Caroline for an extra week.

It was well into the autumn and I was beginning to feel run down, Auntie's letters were worrying me, she was restless and wanted home. Then one day I went down with the measles and landed in the City Hospital for a week. Sister Caroline came in a taxi and took me back. Afterwards I went to see Doctor Rorie who sent me to see Professor Rex Knight, Marischal College, the reason — I was kept in complete ignorance. Shortly I was sent to New Hills Convalescent Home, Bucksburn, for a fortnight. So after three years with the Episcopalian Sisters I took leave of them and journeyed by train to Inverness and went direct to the hotel where Auntie Barbara was regaining her health and strength after a serious illness. Auntie was more than pleased to see me and set about making preparations to return to her wee cottage in the west. I went ahead and boarded the Stratherrick bus en route for Farr, Strathnairn.

CHAPTER 36

THE MONTH, February 1935, saw me back home in Strathnairn, spring was in the air as the flowers struggled with each other to meet the sun's gentle rays and the birds of the air chirping the old glad story, "Spring is here". Auntie Barbara was indeed happy to be home and often watched with interest from the front room window, between lace curtains and pots of fuchsias, and pink and red geraniums, while I toiled in the garden trying to pattern it out. Since her operation Auntie never seemed to regain her strength the same. She sometimes walked as far as the door with the aid of two walking sticks but was for the most part of the day in bed. Nurse Joan Allison, the district's 'Good Samaritan', daily brightened our fireside with her never failing cheery presence. I shall never forget my hasty awakening at four o'clock on Christmas morning. Through the silence of the house broken by the chimes of the old German clock came the desperate cry for help. An icy shudder ran through me. Groping in the dark for the matches I stumbled downstairs with a lighted candle in my hand which shone like a star in the night. My heart turned sick when I beheld Auntie, partly sitting on the commode and clinging to the bed, looking grey and sickly. As I put my arms around her she gasped out, "Lizzie I fear I've taken a stroke". To my dismay she was paralysed down the left side. I eased her gently back into a sitting position and wrapped a blanket round her for oh! she was cold! Regardless of my night attire and bare feet I rushed outside through more than a foot of snow. The snowy stillness was broken by the wailing and screeching of our feathery friends the owls; overhead the stars glittered with a brilliance unusual. Desperate situations demand desperate remedies. Frantically I roused my neighbour and between us we lifted Auntie back into bed and made her as comfortable as we could. There were still a few cinders glowing in the hearth. I threw wood on the fire and the flames shot up while the warmth and light spread through the living-room. I balanced the kettle on and gave Auntie Barbara a good hot stimulant and hot water bottles round about her. Towards the end of July 1936 she grew weaker and I would try to amuse her through the weary hours of a long and tiring day. Some of the old folks from round about would come in for a chat and there was always a cup of tea. Auntie's brother, Archie, from Sockich came east every evening after he had put the cows and stirks to bed and shut the hens in and put the dog in his kennel. Sitting by the blazing hearth he newsed away, now and again taking a draw from his little clay pipe. I remember when, as a child, I used to sit on my wee stoolie and clean out the pipe for him, shredding the Bogie Tobacco with a pen knife, smoothing it between my hands and refilling it. You may be sure I had a draw myself which made me choke and splutter all over the place. I can still hear Auntie Barbara saying, "It serves you right".

August swept in, a season of deep beauty, brushing off here and there a leaf or two. The second week of August, on a Saturday fore-noon, I was occupied with washing draw sheets and was about to hang them out, the day being dry and a good wind blowing, I thought Auntie's words sounded rather strange as she sat propped up in bed, drinking a cup of tea. "You won't be long Lizzie", she said, "No", I replied, "I won't be long". That morning I thought she looked too well for my liking. I was hardly gone five minutes but on entering the room I found her fast asleep and very flushed, her mouth was wide open and she snored loudly. I tried not to think there was anything wrong, little did I know that this was her last sleep. As I stoked the fire up everything was silent as if waiting for something or someone. From afar off came the clarion call of the cock and somewhere a dog barked. One o'clock came and went. I stood still gazing at her and smoothed her silvery hair back and moistened her lips with a little whisky. At last I could stand it no longer and with a sob I fled up to Rose Cottage for Doctor Alick Rose who was at home on holiday. He came with all due haste. After careful examination he lifted her eyelids and said, "Lizzie, I doubt very much if she will ever waken again". "Oh, no!" I cried out in agony as I stood clinging to the bed rail, not daring to move, feeling numb. Recovering myself, I got a telegram sent off to Doctor George Kerr, Inverness, also word to her relatives and Nurse Allison, who shared with me the nursing and all the night watch. During the week that followed there were stormy days and nights of delirium. Hiding my tears as best I could, I bathed Auntie's face and soothed her. In her extreme suffering I prayed for her. Sometimes I lay beside her through the night thinking the feel of my body against hers might relieve or dispel the terror of darkness and loneliness. About three o'clock on Thursday morning, Auntie Barbara rallied for a moment. In my anguish I cried out, "Auntie, it's Lizzie, I'm here, speak to me, please", but Auntie was no longer there to hear me, again she sank into unconsciousness. I was stabbed with pain dreading the loss to come. On Saturday about half past one o'clock while her sister-in-law was reading the Hundred and Twenty-First Psalm, 'I to the hills will lift mine eyes', she stirred. When asked if she could hear it she whispered with her last breath. "Yes". Something like a mist gathered over her countenance and a look of contentment spread over her face and indeed she was beautiful to look upon. I stood in awe, the struggle was over, the veil of the temple was rent for is not the body the temple of the soul which soars back to the Divine Creator who gave it. Understanding of my loss came slowly and I moved away with heavy steps and climbed the stairs to my bedroom which seemed to be tenanted more by the dead than by the living. A hush enfolded the house. Pulling the blinds down I knelt by my bedside. With my face bathed in tears I shivered conscious that my head was throbbing, feeling weak and dazed and weary from the succession of sleepless nights when nurse and I sat by Auntie's bedside Auntie Barbara was eighty-seven years of age and was laid to rest in the family burial ground in Dunlichity Churchyard, the grave is quite near the little Watch-tower. The day of the funeral I was enveloped in loneliness, a complete wretchedness of mind and body swept over me, I was without a home and without a guide to consult in my perplexities. The shock left me weak and shaken, my nerves seemed raw and exposed. I could have stayed on in the house as I was offered work in Farr House by Mrs MacKenzie's housekeeper, Bertha. Before Auntie died I made up my mind to work in a Nursing Home for incurable patients to try and enhance my education, cutting myself off from a hard and relentless world for which I was so wretchedly ill-equipped and unfitted. Auntie's oldest brother, Angus Fraser, from Crown Street, Inverness, offered me a home and the little money that was left over after all the funeral expenses were paid. I felt it would be nothing more or less than a jumping off place so I was not going to be dependent on charity. Going out, I took a last look round for indeed I was leaving the place where I was reared and nourished since the age of seven. I listened to the song of the birds and the rustle of the leaves, wearily I made my way back to the house where Auntie's relatives were waiting. That afternoon I seemed to have stepped out of the world as the door of Eastern Cottage closed behind me. Perhaps if I had seen the whole pattern of my life I would not have gone forward but it is beyond man's power to change one's destiny. For over the next three months I stayed with Auntie Barbara's niece in Castle Street, Inverness. During that time I visited Doctor Ian MacLeod who tried to persuade me not to do anything rash. I was as stubborn as a mule, nothing he said would induce me to change my mind.

CHAPTER 37

DURING MY stay with Auntie Barbara's niece I came in contact with a member of a religious party who, in her own way, was trying to be helpful, so on the night before my departure I was issued with an address. The date was 18th December, 1936. I journeyed down south to a Nursing Home for incurable patients in Hawick where people of all denominations were admitted into this highly efficient institution. The staff, I was convinced were angels of mercy, and I hoped to improve under their Christian instruction and further my education I was well warned it would be no easy task that lay ahead of me, also I was free to go at any time being only on trial. On my arrival at the Home I was given a spontaneous welcome by the Sister-in-Charge who exclaimed, "Oh what a lovely Christmas box", and little wonder for they were short-handed.

The nursing home was a two-storey building with a spacious front hall. On the ground floor was a large ward used for holiday guests and convalescants, also there were a few private sick rooms. There was an old fashioned wooden lift for the use of the patients, this was manoeuvred by pulling the ropes up and down by hand. Upstairs there were three wards, two of which were occupied by patients. In the centre was a small Chapel, one of the walls constructed like sliding doors, a surprising piece of work and craftsmanship. This gave admittance to two of the wards, the beds were arranged so that the invalids could take part in religious Service. The silence of the building was broken by repeated prayers and occasional cries and groans from the sick, some of whom had spinal and hip disease. Others suffered from shock and were unable to speak, one woman was curled up like a winkle her knees almost touching her chin with acute rheumatoid arthritis. There was also one ailing diabetic and one blind person. They were all burdened with some incurable disease or other. A physician attended daily. For a while I slept in the caretaker's house, which was adjacent to the Nursing Home through a long glass conservatory. Soon I learned the rules and was employed in different kinds of work. I regarded those in charge with great respect and as in a state of sanctity.

In the month of February 1937 a flu epidemic raged. Short-handed though they were and half the nursing staff laid up, they braved the elements doing a humane job of work attending to the sick and dying. Often when polishing a ward or cleaning a sick room I was taken away to start on something else, thus being prevented from applying myself to one job for any length of time. All this I meekly carried out with unquestioning obedience. From half past four in the morning till after ten o'clock my body was kept in a constant state of activity and exertion. I usually found myself exhausted and fighting down waves of nausea, which rose within me, but I continued uncomplaining, the making of the beds and helping with the sick and the usual chores. Doing my best was only a minimum of efficiency, always with the feeling of being watched from some observation post. Every night before retiring it was my duty to see to the hot water bottles for three of the wards, after which I helped to wash up in the scullery. It was one of those evenings when carrying a pile of plates from the kitchen, without warning, they crashed to the floor. My left arm seemed to go limp and to my utter dismay turned black to the fingertips. I stood gazing at it for a few moments and then to my profound relief Mother Nature stepped in and restored it back to normal. I then set to work with renewed vigour. That night, my head swimming with sleep, I staggered upstairs when a tide of dizziness swept over me and gripping the banister I overcame it with great difficulty. One morning the situation was brought to a climax, when I could hardly manage the lift, I felt faint and sick and everytime I pulled the rope, the wooden cage turned black and began to recede gently from me. There were two patients inside leaning against the wall for support. I summoned up every ounce of strength and brought it safely to the ground floor. My face bathed in perspiration; amidst the ceaseless routine of the day, I doubted if I could go on much longer. I saw myself a failure drifting with no ambition down and out, tracing my footsteps through life with nothing to live for. One evening I went in search of the Sister-in-Charge and made known my request that I be relieved of my duties and convalesce for a little while to bring my strength up to standard and find a light post. The Sister promised to speak to the Superior about the matter. While talking to her I felt uncomfortable and ill at ease, suddenly my eyesight seemed to go, everything kept going out of focus. "Sister, Sister, I can't see," I cried out in alarm, "Don't leave me please". I began to take those turns frequently, especially on rising in the mornings, I would have to sit down for a while until it passed over. I had already seen the local Doctor who gave me iron pills which had little effect on my illness. During that period the Home was given more helpers, four young girls. As for the lift the caretaker was summoned in. He remarked to me that it took him all his time to haul it up and down. It was some time before I saw the Superior who informed me I wasn't to work so hard, promising to do what she could, knowing I had nowhere to go or no one to care for me. I remember her words as if they were yesterday, "I'll see that you have some place where you can rest for a while and get well", she remarked. "Thank you", I said taking leave. I continued with my daily chores which were made a bit lighter.

The month being July 1937 the day arrived for me to leave the Nursing Home. One of the Sisters to my amazement was weeping and said it would be better if I were dead. I didn't understand her and I was too ill to care. I had not been informed as to where I was going. Accompanied by one of the guests, I journeyed to Edinburgh where I was conducted to my unknown destination. This experience, stark and vivid in it's intensity is printed indelibly on my mind.

Coronation Year 1937

Edinburgh the capital of Scotland with its fortress towering high on a rock of great size, a haunted Castle steeped in history with an air of mystery wrapped in mystery and clothed in ancient grandeur speaks and breathes of strange romances and tragedies. Here Scottish justice is still administered, From it roars the perfect cast of the turbulent past of a discarded brat.

CHAPTER 38

THIRTEENTH JULY, Monday: I was dumped amongst a group of well trained teenagers in the junkyard of no ordinary house where to hear was to obey. I arrived during their recreation hour, they were standing and sitting around analysing each other. Well, there I was, what was left of me, a mere shadow of my former self and it certainly was a some- what strange place in which to convalesce but, nevertheless, a roof over my head. We are here to do the little we can the best we can. Evidently this was the best that was done for me. Instead of stimulating me it had a most depressing effect and gave me the jitters. Nothing seemed to be real any more. I was sent to work in the laundry, also given a clumsy bucket and made to go down on my knees and scrub stone passages, feeling as if my inside was coming through the walls of my stomach. When spoken to I could not answer except by tears. They over-estimated my strength, my body was not exactly made of volcano rock. You cannot draw blood out of a stone. Steeped in loneliness, eating my soul out, I wept bitterly. Lengthy daily prayers broke the afternoon tasks, one of the many penances together with my bodily pain and depression of mind and the rules of silence which were scrupu- lously obeyed brought me to a state which I cannot describe. Every night we filed upstairs, a long female procession, I almost groaned. A deadly chill of fear and foreboding shot through me as the key turned in the lock. Gazing out of the dormitory window across this ancient city of moving lights which kindled and gleamed forth in the dusk, my thoughts strayed back and I visualised myself once again a little girl hurrying off to school, my school bag slung over my shoulder, the milk can in my hand, skipping along east the road drinking in the ever sweet changing countryside. Once more I hear the echo of Auntie Barbara's voice full of anxiety calling, "Lizzie are you there?" but, alas, no more would I hear that beloved voice.

On rising in the mornings I fell back across the bed in an effort to dress myself. Worn out in a semi-comatose state I kept asking for a Doctor but always got the same answer, "the doctor will come as soon as he can" which increased the anxiety I already felt. Seemingly it was beyond their experience to understand when a person needed medical aid. The organisation in this place, from my point of view, was all wrong and there was no one big enough to put it right. On the Friday afternoon, during the lengthy prayers, suddenly a blackness curled up in front of me and I felt myself pitch forward. Before passing out I heard those words, "Oh we know what's wrong with her." I'm afraid I was sadly misjudged. On regaining consciousness I found myself lying on the floor in a daze of exhaustion and strain. I cried out for water but no one saw or heard me. I was left helpless at the mercy of my grief. Like the sands of time my hours were running out and I knew if I did not take prompt action I would not survive much longer. Along came Saturday and, after a wakeful night, I felt increasingly ill. Breakfast was brought to me in bed. The food, in my opinion, was insufficient to maintain bodily vigour. I again enquired about a Doctor. I began to feel that they thought I was half-witted. Later on I rose, dressed and went downstairs. Going out into the garden I was pushed violently in the back and addressed in those terms, "Hey you, go and do some weeding". I was aghast at the vulgar impudence of the woman with a bunch of keys jingling by her side. She was strong and sturdy and managed to keep a good face on life without frills and looking the picture of rubicund health. I wept like a child being punished when it had no memory of doing any wrong. From the depth of despair I cried out to my Divine Creator that if it be His will to deliver me from those who now surrounded me. Suddenly I remembered five words, "Oh ye of little faith". Overcome by mental tiredness I deposited myself on the ground to sleep it off after which I took stock of my bearings for I had planned before another day passed over my head I would be gone forever from this spider's web. All through the night I gave the matter considerable thought for all was one ghastly mistake which I could not figure out. Slowly the first grey light of dawn seeped through the window. It was Sunday, 19th July, when I planned to escape that evening. The hours seemed to drag and twice I was in a semi-comatose state and was continually drinking and passing water. At last the long day came to an end and everyone filed into prayers. Lingering behind, taking all precautions I slipped outside. With the evening dusk the song of the birds faded to a silence. I prayed and hoped I would not take another attack on the way as I fled across the narrow strip of ground which revealed itself, a patch of grass, shrubs and trees, and at the west side of the building I noticed an open window where someome was peeling potatoes. I crept further back or else I should have been observed. I paused, crouching close to the ground, sick and shivering, taking advantage of the cover afforded by the trees for fear I might be detected. Guided by my strong sense of direction I began to work my way round from one tree trunk to another. Suddenly, I reached a part of the grounds where the wall was lower. My legs trembling as if they might give way at any moment I leaned against a tree for support and closed my eyes and prayed to God for guidance through the reefs and shoals of that sea of misery. Gathering up my strength and looking around I saw no one there. I put my foot into a niche of the wall and hauled myself up and peered cautiously over the top. I saw the long dusty road ahead, opposite a row of bungalows, nearby was a tennis court, a lad and a lass were engaged in a game of tennis, their voices rippled with laughter. I lost no time and waving my arms called to them to help me. They were so close it was impossible to believe that they neither saw nor heard me for they gave no answering signal and turned away without making any pretence of helping me. Growing breathless I felt the venture was too great. My plight during those seconds lent precision to my mind so that my thoughts went racing ahead to escape from this shuddering misery. Once more I took a quick look back over my shoulder, listening one minute, two minutes, but all was impressive stillness. Struggling up into a more flexible position I swung my legs over the wall. It was for all the world like a Punch and Judy Show as I slithered down the steep incline like a puppet whose strings had all been released at once, the sandy bank crumbling as I fell. Exhausted by exertions and the shock of my fall, I lay where I had fallen for a few moments until my strength returned and my spirits rose. I gave a contented sigh — so far so good. Suddenly my attention was arrested by the pitter patter of footsteps coming towards me. My heart thudded, slowly I turned my head and stared incredulously at a little round-eyed fair haired lassie between four and five years of age who looked curious and impressed, her dolly cuddled in her arms. "Hello", I said giving her a half-hearted smile and, as I struggled to my feet, she held out her tiny hand to help me. Overcome with gratitude, mingling with astonishment, my eyes suddenly welled up with tears as I gave her my hand and allowed her to guide me. Surely it must have been an act of Providence that sent this child across my path. At that precise moment those words flashed across my mind, "A little child shall lead them" linked with, "Oh ye of little faith". The good little Samaritan gently led me to the end bungalow. There I was confronted by her mother who did not seem in the least taken aback by my sudden appearance and dishevelled look. Stumbling in my speech I begged her pardon for my intrusion. The warmth of her welcome moved me deeply and put to flight any misgivings. She was gentle and kind and asked no questions but said in a quiet way, "You won't be the first to come over that wall". Seated before a fire the good woman spread a spotless cloth on the table and on it put all the food from her cupboard and pressed me to eat as hostess to guest. She was being neighbourly to the one in need because it was part of her nature to do so giving her labours gratuitously which is the application of real goodness to common life.

After I had eaten and drunk several cups of tea I was more able to think what to do next. I decided to call in the nearest vicarage and see the clergyman and put my case before him. As I rose to go my eyes fell on my clothes, knowing I wouldn't get very far in this rig out. My hostess, guessing my thoughts, arrayed me in one of her own coats, brown with a fur collar attached to the neck, also a felt hat which she pulled down over my eyes making me feel like a sleuth on the prowl. I was profoundly grateful for the sudden and unexpected assistance. Noticing my restiveness she said, "I will see you through the streets". Taking my arm she clasped my hand in hers, this added greatly to my comfort. Arriving at the vicarage I was ushered into the presence of the minister, whereupon my hostess on taking leave of me held out her hand. Forcing back the tears that welled in my eyes I thanked her for the great service she had rendered me. At the same time I remembered those words, "In as much as ye have done it unto one of the least of these my brethren. ye have done it unto Me". Left alone with the company I had difficulty in expressing myself. The lack of sleep and the emotional strain to which I had been subjected in those past days had drained my life-stream and taken toll of my nerves. The interview lasted only a few minutes. The gentleman kindly gave me an address of a little mission run by a religious body. I set out, footsore and utterly

Above: Dr Alexander Rose, a dear friend since childhood, pictured outside his home, Rose Cottage, Farr.

Dr Rose again, pictured at the side of Rose Cottage, ready for his favourite pastime of gardening or to help in the corn fields.

Eastern Cottage, Farr, where I spent seven of the happiest years of my childhood days.

'Auntie' Barbara Fraser of Eastern Cottage, Farr, Strathnairn, where I was boarded out by the Edinburgh Parish Council whose offices are still in Castle Terrace. She gave me a true home and I shall always be indebted to her for her kind and motherly guidance.

weary. On my arrival I was admitted into a waiting room where I saw one of the staff. Somehow I seemed to stutter in my speech. They were very kind and gave me a cup of tea and buttered bread. After I had eaten they informed me I could not stay there as there was no room, which reminded me of the words, "There was no room in the Inn". On hearing this my heart almost turned over in my body and I became cold and sick. Presently another of the staff entered the waiting-room and said I had no further need to worry about my safety as she was now ready to conduct me to a place of refuge where I would be looked after and receive medical aid. As I plodded along by her side, rubbing shoulders with the crowds of people drifting leisurely to and fro I tried my utmost to look on the bright side and to master the leaden pain at my left breast. We spoke little, suddenly the tone of her voice changed and struck a fear into me, lighting the fuse as it were. My heart thumped sickeningly and I felt myself getting nervy and suspicious. I prayed and hoped that my suspicions were unfounded but little did I know that the nights work was far from completed.

CHAPTER 39

ON REACHING my destination in the High Street we climbed a narrow stairway which was very dimly lit. Here I dropped anchor and was treated with unusual courtesy by a young woman whom I took to be one of the staff. "You're looking simply exhausted, let me help you to bed", she said. After what I had been through that day I was glad of her assistance. "Thank you for being so kind to me", I said, "Please I've got to have a Doctor", I cried distractedly. "He has already been sent for and will be here any moment". she replied. Wearily I lay down and slept with my ears open. How long I'd been lying there I do not know but suddenly I opened my eyes and sat bolt upright as it were on tenterhooks for, on glancing around, I seemed to be in a windowless room while here and there holy pictures hung on the walls and a holy statue stood on a nearby table. I stared and stared. It can't be true I thought dizzily as my head cleared. The whole place looked like a small chapel and my heart sank in fear. As for the Doctor he never came as was promised. "Oh God, help me!" I moaned, there is nobody who cares. My throat was parched. If only I could get a drink of water. I also wanted to get some idea of my whereabouts and, as I dragged myself out of the bed, shivering uncontrollably, I looked at the door with the dreadful thought in my mind that it might be locked. I approached somewhat unsteadily on my feet and turned the handle, a shock of relief surged through me when it opened. I stepped forward and crept along the dimly lit corridor then turning the corner saw a thin line of light under a closed door. I stood hesitatingly, picking up courage, and knocked gently. It was immediately opened by a stern looking woman with a mop of hair as black as a raven who eyed me with extreme disfavour. Trembling I stammered out "I am very sorry to disturb you but please may I have a drink of cold water, I am so thirsty?" Assuming the high tone of authority, "You had better go back to bed and I will bring it to you", she said. "Thank you, I will", and I shuffled off miserably. In no time she appeared with a glass of water. While I was quenching my thirst I asked her why the Doctor didn't come. "Oh there must have been some mistake", she said carefully, as if repeating a phrase. A certain woman's name was mentioned when I arrived, the same name I heard spoken of in the Nursing Home who ran such an establishment as this, I wondered if it could be the one and the same person. To satisfy my curiosity I said, "Does this place belong to a Miss Rutherford?" She looked startled, her eyes like slits, and as watchfully, I imagined, as a spider balancing beautifully at the centre of its web. In a clipped tone she asked, "Is it this one or the one before?" She wheeled about and was gone from the room giving me no chance to reply. The mask was perfect but no doubt it was intended for my good. I was having no more wool pulled over my eyes and at all costs I had to get out of this entanglement for I felt I was lured into a deliberate trap which I proved later on without the shadow of a doubt. Having been reared in the Highlands I wasn't such a bad trapper myself and was determined somehow to outwit them. I lay there quietly nerving myself with the thought of escape. Slowly I emerged from my cocoon and dressed myself. My hat I carried in my hand. It was no easy moment for me as I opened the door and peered into the corridor. The silence was uncanny and with a soft tread I moved cautiously almost suffocating with breathlessness and dreading that I should make the faintest rustle. The floor creaked as I trod on loose boards. Cold terror crept over me, half expecting to feel a hand lunge out at me. Suddenly I reached what looked to be the main door. This end of the passage was almost in total darkness. Sliding my hands over the door I felt for the lock and fumbled about with it as quietly as possible trying to unlock it with complete lack of success. I was beginning to come to the end of my patience. Weariness and a sense of failure overswept me, tears of weakness and distress poured down my face. I grew desperate and made a last final attempt but only succeeded in making a noise. I heard a slight movement and started nervously, feeling the nearness of evil. I dropped my hat, there was no time to retrieve it. Moving swiftly I opened the nearest door and mechanically my hand went to the electric switch and pressed it down. The light spread itself over articles of furniture showing it was a sitting-room. My eye fell on the window, the blind was up. Almost simultaneously a closer sound arrested my attention. Someone was coming stealthily towards me. In one continuous unbroken movement I leapt towards the window and with a slight push of my hands, it shot up like lightning and in a flash I thrust myself out head-first, landing on the sill. Looking down below I got a shock which I cannot describe. I found myself at a point of critical importance, plunged into which yet seemed unavoidable. I heard a gasp behind me. To my profound relief below the sill I observed a nice piece of foot-work which would have taxed a mountain goat's agility. This way I made my miraculous escape

For the next few minutes I lived in sheer terror. I planted my feet firmly on the narrow wooden ledge which extended some distance along the building to the left. Every person has his own reason for living and dying, I wanted to live or perish in the attempt. I braced myself against the wall, desperation driving me on. Balancing myself with the greatest of difficulty, hesitancy, terrified that I would take a one-way ticket. Death was not on my doorstep yet. My courage was swift and unerring, indeed I had not expected to make such rapid progress. I suddenly came to an abrupt halt beside a window of the adjoining house where I clung grimly to a drain pipe. I was in a horrible dilemma and I was petrified into stillness while around me was wrapped in slumber. Down below shone shimmering lights of varied colours. All that I was worried about was how to get down but the question no sooner posed itself than suddenly out of the shadows appeared the arm of the law looking like a small dwarf in Policeman's uniform while I stood like a phantom, an amazing spectacle, perched on a terrifying lofty ledge forty feet above the High Street. The street lamps gleamed forth like drops of gold giving it the dismal scene of a stage effect. Desperately I called out, "Help, Help, Help". Looking up the poor man wondered what was afoot. Suddenly his deep melodious voice floated upwards, "Mercy me lassie, what are you doing up there?" "I can't explain now, please help me", I shouted down. He replied, "I am off duty now and on my way home". Like a miracle the nearby window went up with a sudden abruptness and out popped a woman's head and relieved the drama. "In Heaven's name come inside", she cried out in alarm. I hesitated, the Policeman's voice again floated upwards, "For pity's sake go in lassie", his voice full of concern for my safety. "Only on condition that you will protect me and not force me back where I've just escaped from", I cried in desperation. "I give you my word of honour no harm will come to you, now, please go in", he said. I was sorry for the woman, I saw she was worried at me standing out there. She assisted me into the room and I sat down on a chair. Looking up into her face I said, "Please may I have a drink of water". "Certainly", she said, and handed me a cup of water, I almost grabbed it from her, drinking it greedily. By this time the Constable was on his way up. As he came in I said to them both, "I'm sorry but my behaviour does seem to call for a little explanation. I've only been a few hours next door but during that time I felt myself being held a prisoner. I cannot explain any more, please accept my statement." "All right lassie", he said. His kindly look and words went home. I thanked them both. The scene ended. I made my way downstairs and stepped out on to the pavement. Giving a deep sigh I was free again! My nervous tension eased and my muscles relaxed and I trudged slowly along the High Street. But, alas, little did I know that before the day ended a similar experience would evolve.

CHAPTER 40

IN THE clear cold air of the early hours of the morning of 20th July, 1937, I found it difficult to decide what to do; no friends, no home — a poor weary stranger, as I plodded through the deserted tram-lined streets like a shadow revisiting by night the scenes of former days. The lamplights flickered one by one while now and again I passed down the side streets and alleyways. What appeared to be dustbins loomed up beside the kerb, the silence was uncanny. Suddenly a door opened, a figure tottered out, paused for a moment and stared at me, dropped something into the gutter and shuffled off into the house leaving an unpleasant odour of alcohol behind. I found myself walking in the direction of Dean Village. I hardly knew why I was going there for I was likely to get a cold reception. From afar off a clock chimed out the hour. The sky was like black velvet dusted with countless stars and as I drew nearer and closer to the village my knees almost giving way and, fearing I should fall, I paused for a few moments. I leaned heavily against the railings and watched the rushing torrents ot old Father Dean remembering once again with a pang the many dreary nights I lay nestled to its side. How strange the phases of our lives that pass and are gone! I also remembered my Papa and tears blinded my eyes trickling down my cheeks.

As I turned away my aunt's house loomed up in front of me. I felt sick at heart for the next few moments were to be like a nightmare. The living room window was partly open. I gently tapped on the pane — all was silence. Pulling it down I hauled myself on to the sill and desperately called out, "Auntie, its Lizzie, please may I come in?" whereupon she rose and opened the door, a slight pause indicating. "What brings you here?" "I'm sorry Auntie to trouble you at this hour of the morning but I've been wandering about". I felt too dazed to think of a suitable excuse and it was obvious that the true reason must remain unknown. She beckoned me in. A few beer bottles stood on the table near the bed, beer was trickling down on to the floor from an overturned glass. The air reeked with the smell and the lighted gas was at its lowest peep. My throat hurt but I dared not ask for a cup of tea. She tumbled in over the bed mumbling under her breath while I crouched down by the dying embers of the fire. At last, without undressing, I crept in over the back of the bed and lay down. I must have dozed for when I woke the room was bathed in sunshine. Auntie staggered from her bed, put the kettle on, made tea and handed me a cup which I gulped down. She then told me I couldn't stay there and advised me to go to the workhouse. With never a word I dragged myself from the bed and humbly thanked her for allowing me to stay the night. She then showed me the door, outside an old woman stood by. With my head bowed down and shoulders haunched I staggered like a drunken woman up the cobbled brae I overheard those words, "Well, well, that surely is the MacKay family skeleton". Nearing the top of the brae I was in a semi-comatose condition. A man came out of the nearby garage and I overheard him say to his mate, "She seems to be in a pretty bad way". Suddenly I felt their kindly hands assist me into a taxi, my senses seemed to be slipping away. When I came round I discovered I was in the Infirmary. I was given a glass of milk and biscuits. Feeling better I thanked them and finally rose to go for I had to see about my few modest belongings. On the way I met a Policeman and enquired where the Police Station was. Putting my case before them I was informed that I would have to retrieve my own belongings as it was out of their jurisdiction. Sickening pain stabbed me through, my feet seemed heavily weighted so that it was an effort to move them and I shuffled along like an old withered crony. Taking a firm grip of myself, for I seemed to be going round in circles without knowing it, I found myself in Princes Street and had just gone a little way when I stopped a passer-by and begged twopence. Believe me, my cheeks burned with shame for I did not relish the thought of having to beg in the streets. Boarding a tram car I alighted at the West End and wandered down Queensferry Street. I looked around to see if I could find somewhere I could sit down and rest, footsore and weary I dragged myself down a side street. Coming to a church I went in and knelt in the nave. The vastness and silence were healing to me. Feverishly I repeated the Lord's Prayer and feeling more rested I rose to go. Like an arrow a certain name flashed across my mind, a Miss Archibald who lived here, whom I had met in St. Margaret's Convent, Aberdeen. Where in Edinburgh she lived I hadn't the faintest clue but I made my way to the Post Office in Queensferry Street. There was just a possibility that her name would be listed in the telephone book. Mr MacKay, the Postmaster, gave me the 'phone book. I flipped over the pages and ran my fingers down the close print where I found her name and address and I discovered she was within walking distance. A few minutes later I reached her flat in Drumsheugh Gardens and rang the bell. The door was opened by the lady herself who was in the act of going out. Stumbling for words, I said, "I'm Lizzie, you remember me, we met in Aberdeen". "Yes, of course, Lizzie I remember you quite well, do come in", she said. I gave her a brief outline of the predicament I was in. She was kindness itself and assured me she would do all in her power to help. "You are very good, I cannot thank you enough", I said. Before leaving the flat she adjusted the collar of my coat and taking my arm in a possessive sort of way she shepherded me through the streets. I was vaguely conscious of vehicles and figures floating past.

CHAPTER 41

BEFORE THE evening shadows deepened I found myself in a house in the north side of Edinburgh, 18 Dean Terrace. I remember with some pain and bewilderment that first evening, I was seized with uneasiness. Shortly after I arrived I was shown my bedroom which was right at the very top of the building. On coming down stairs I followed my hostess into a sort of dining room, a chair was drawn up at the table. She motioned me to sit down, a tight-lipped woman clattered in with a steaming plate and a chunk of bread. "Your supper", she said and clapped it down on the table. "Thank you kindly", I murmured and nibbled uneasily for I was more thirsty than hungry. The food seemed to stick half way in my throat and I coughed and spluttered all over the place breaking out into a sweat, tears streaming down my face. How I longed for tenderness and consolation. The pangs of loneliness and suffering are beyond my powers of description.

Having partaken of a little food I was immediately summoned to a small room with rows of coarse looking benches where evening prayers were held. Afterwards I was reminded it was time for me to retire. I bade them goodnight. Going out into the hall two people were standing at the front door breathing in God's air, for indeed it was a heavenly evening. Ascending the stairs I overheard someone speaking on the telephone. "Oh, they are coming to take her back in the morning". Lingering a moment I looked back over my shoulder just as she replaced the receiver. Reaching the third storey I noticed a door standing ajar. The room looked like a dormitory there were rows of beds. Feeling somewhat puzzled I climbed the rest of the stairs. On entering the small bedroom, my night attire was laid out and the bed clothes folded back Slipping off my clothes I donned myself in a long white nightdress. Casting my eyes round the room I stood as silent as the grave, my eyes glued to the door, for I was seeing something I had never seen before, a square hole in the centre and iron bars across it. The room also revealed a closed skylight window which also had iron bars, the only means of light and air. Doubts passed through my mind in dreary chilling succession. I suddenly shrunk back into myself with fear. What I had overheard on my way upstairs told me all I wanted to know. Apparently they were making a thorough job of it. I was fooled, for a threat to my whole existence was at stake. Some people's promises are a little misleading. They had everything successfully launched, whether it would go according to plan was another matter. The battle was about to commence as all other battles in my life. I was finding them fiercer as the years went by.

I descended the stairs very lightly until I reached the next flight when I was stopped by the low murmur of voices from down below. My heart pounded furiously. Nearby a door stood partly open, I crept forward and listened intently for some sound but the silence told me that there was nobody there. A clock in the house somewhere began to chime musically. I moved cautiously, treading softly, and pushed wider the open door. The room was empty. I stepped in and glanced wearily around, it was a large room and looked like a lounge. It was unlighted save by the transparent sky. There were two French windows — my mind working fast. I had the rudiments of a plan. It was I who would decide for the dramatic moment to arrive as I sped noiselessly over the carpeted floor while vestiges of light from the summer night fell about me making me seem like a ghost. Approaching one of the French windows I turned the handle and glided out onto the balcony with the watchful eyes of Heaven above me. I trusted to a generous Providence, for a split second I stood motionless, undecided as to my course of action. Suddenly I threw myself on the sympathy of the public and cried out for help, my voice soaring past the limit of inaudibility. People going to and fro, attracted by my cries, gathered in little knots and before long I had quite a gallery. While I stood betwixt Heaven and the earth, perched three storeys high, a melancholy spectacle, or perhaps I should say like a sheeted spectre, one in a multitude, yet one all alone like one who had strayed from the populace graveyard. Murmurs of sympathy floated upwards.

In front of me the gardens might have been a painted picture while I drooped like a flower out of water under the glowing embers of a late summer evening. The tense crowd now gathered and were transfixed like figures in a wax show, giving a stage effect, for from the distance came echoes of voices singing without words — bringing sound and picture together. Silence, like clamour, is catching and the audience waited expectantly for the next act. There was something that drove me on, that made me afraid to linger. I moved quickly and silently and gave a demonstration of my school-days and with startling abruptness I vaulted over the railings into the next balcony. Almost simultaneously, Miss Archibald appeared in the danger zone, the deadlock for the moment was complete between my pursuer and myself. Now she knew, any enterprising move on her part would provide the startling

110

gong, and as she coaxed me, I felt a curious warning which held me off. I was becoming quite familiar with the arts of deception and a pretty good judge in a case of this kind. Since then, I have learned to accept friendship with precaution. The whole procedure was like a nursery game in which I was to play the major role.

The crowd was fascinated by the prospect of what was really going to happen. Escape was cut off in either direction, everyone was at action stations and all were petrified into silence. It was I again who would decide when the dramatic moment would arrive, I knew the time was close. The scene swam before my eyes, the stage was set for the entrance. I gently tapped on the window near me hoping someone would appear. I listened but there was no answer. I pressed my face close to the pane, the house seemed dreary and deserted, committing a breach of the peace was my only salvation — attracting the police. In a matter of seconds, strung out though they were, I still had one minute to go before zero hour, I had made up my mind as to my course of action. With renewed vigour and growing desperation I gathered up my strength and with both hands smashed the thick plated glass of the French window. A hush fell over the crowd; breathing heavily from exertion, and in panicky haste, I pushed my head and shoulders through the gap, the jagged ends of broken glass pierced through my nightdress. The predicament in which I now found myself was a fresh phase in the pattern of events. I tramped barefooted on the pieces of glass, strewn about like a jig-saw puzzle. Entering the room I realised with a pang of terror that there was no place to hide, its furniture was shrouded in white dust sheets and it looked for all the world like a morgue. I felt as if a bucket of water had been emptied over me, not with water but with fear. As I tried to withdraw into a corner I was checked by the sudden entrance of two women with, I thought, puppet-like wooden smiles as their hands snaked out and gripped me round the upper arm. I was beaten; they had won

111

the second round. The two women looked at one another evidently thinking I had become slightly insane and said, "She looks exhausted", yet I was anything but in the last stages of physical exhaustion. They retreated warily downstairs with me, to a casual observer it might have seemed that they were supporting a drunken woman. The front door was open and I was surrounded by faces and faces. The silence was excruciatingly intense. Little did they know I was preparing to stage a last act. (A person off balance is a person defeated.) Taking them completely by surprise I thrust aside the two women, almost overturning them as they backpedalled into the front hall. (One will run hard for reward but a lot harder for fear.) I was grateful for the way the people parted and made no attempt to stop me. Fear lent me wings; I heard the soft compassionate murmurings of a woman as I raced off at top speed, congratulating myself on my dramatic escape. After running about one hundred yards I paused indecisively and my eyes scanned the terrace and rested on a closed car drawn up on the left hand side of the terrace parked there it appeared for my convenience. At first I saw it without actually perceiving it then something seemed to snap in my mind. Suddenly I was very much aware of the arm of the law standing alongside the kerb by the van. With a sob, I dashed across and clung to him for protection, "Please, please take me with you, don't send me back to that house", I cried distractedly. His face full of compassion, said, "We will have to take you back to get your clothes", whereupon he assisted me into the van which drove the short distance, while he remained my fears subsided. I was conscious of being very tired after that exciting scene and my throat felt uncomfortably hot. Three or four women stood by as the policeman helped me to dress, their looks were unsympathetic. They were part of the general landscape and of the number of those who refused to hear my desperate plea for understanding and help. They were people with whom my mind could find no point of contact. As I watched, fascinated, listening with unspeakable horror, it was like watching them play a part as they misconstrued the facts to the police, wishing me to be certified insane, and locked up in the hour of my victory. I recoiled in horror. It was abundantly clear that they were doing the thinking for me and expecting their imperative orders to be obeyed. This, indeed, was subtle revenge. In indignant protest against the stupidity of their words my whole soul rose up in accusation of them. I was in possession of my faculties while they were not; my mechanism was not out of order and I didn't need to be put into the repair yard. The whole conspiracy was marvellously defeated, for a stronger will than theirs had spoken and stilled their tongues. A little noisy speech uttered, then dead and gone for ever. God will one day speak out words that cannot be misunderstood. Such people by exceeding their authority could cause unnecessary suffering and pain to others.

CHAPTER 42

THE POLICEMAN, a gentleman, calm and self-controlled, a man of firmness and independence of mind, took care of the matter right away and saved me from what might well have been a disaster. He looked at me with much gentleness and took the hurt from the others' words. On examining my hands and bare feet he was amazed to find what a miraculous escape I had, there wasn't so much as a scratch to be seen. What we want in this world is more patience and more understanding, one ought to try to make patients better not worse and, indeed, the enormity of their error must have struck them for they mumbled words of apology but giving me a hard stare. I lurched unsteadily into the police car and now I was where those quick authoritative hands could not reach me. The scene ended.

From there I was delivered up in an unceremonial fashion to the police headquarters into whose custody I was taken pending further enquiries. All particulars were taken, expert hands travelled over my clothes. With the arm of the law leading the way and a wardress behind me, I was conducted along the stone corridor, coming to an abrupt halt where a massive door stood wide open. As I staggered in I heard the door clang to and the turning of the great key.

Gazing around I saw high above a skylight window with iron bars across it. I observed the floor sloping slightly, also there was a lavatory, the light wasn't bad. Feeling sick and dizzy I lay down on the bare boards of my cell, attempting with sleep to blot out my whirling thoughts for in the past hours I had encountered incredible difficulties, an innocent figure, sadly misjudged, I languished on the floor of my jail. Lying there looking like something dramatised made in to an exciting play with a dramatic cast behind which brings to mind a film "Limelight" and the worlds greatest comedian the one and only Charlie Chaplin completing his final major role, forlorn and lovelorn languishing on the floor of his prison cell with the theme from the sound track to help to alleviate his mental depression. My world shrank to the size of my cell window, I was at low ebb but felt the tide rising. My throat was sore and burned with a furious thirst for water. I could hear the policeman on night duty walking to and fro so, struggling to my feet I knocked on the door. Instantly a face loomed up in front of me, "Please may I have a blanket, I feel so cold and clammy and, please may I have a drink of water and a Bible?" I asked the policeman, whereupon he immediately fetched both. After I had gulped down the water he kindly tucked the blanket round my miserable body and soothed me. At intervals during the night I cried out "Water, water" which he sometimes pushed through the grille of the prison door, sometimes the policeman came in with it. Once, gazing up into his face I said, "You will let me stay here, you won't send me back in the morning?" Placing his hand on my head he assured me they couldn't send anyone back against their will. In the morning I felt chilled and stretched

out my cramped limbs. The policeman served me with breakfast, porridge and milk, morning rolls with a layer of sausage
between and a steaming mug of tea. Will I ever forget that
experience — no, not as long as I live — The great big man
knelt down on one knee and gently laid the tray on my lap
but, alas, fatigue had conquered my appetite, tears blurred
my eyes and try as I would the food refused to go over my
aching throat. Later on a wardress came in and gently helped
me from my cell floor and guided me to a toilet where I
washed and combed my hair, "You are not going to send
me back?" I asked. "No", she said but some people did call
about eight o'clock in the morning with a van but the police
authorities refused to hand you over. Relief mingled with
gratitude surged through me.

The next minute I found myself in the courtroom. I took
my stand in the witness box in front of the magistrate who
bade me to be seated. The hearing opened. His Lordship then
read out the tragic nature of the charges against me — "That
on the twentieth July, just after midnight, you were perched
forty feet on a narrow ledge above the High Street and, on
the same day, between the hours of nine and ten o'clock p.m.
you did commit a breach of the peace in Dean Terrace. Do
you admit to those charges?" he asked. Numb though I was
I answered "Yes". No further questions were asked. They
had made the diagnosis and the diet was deserted and I was
not convicted.

Then I was conducted upstairs to another portion of the
building looking like a miniature arena with a partition of
iron railings across the entire centre with a door in the middle.
The heavy iron door swung open as I entered and my eyes
fell on a bed with a red cover, a table and chair stood near.
In a matter of seconds the prison doctor appeared. His
trained eye told him all he wanted to know without going
any further, "Why didn't you have a doctor before now?" he
enquired. "It wasn't for the want of asking, for it was my
constant plea during the last six days" I answered. "Would

you be quite willing to go to Craiglockhart Hospital?" he asked. I gratefully said, "Yes". At that precise moment a Miss Russell, whom I met in Aberdeen, came in and we spoke to one another as one would speak to an old friend.

Leaving the police station we journeyed to the Parish Council, Castle Terrace, where the poor doctor was in authority to direct as he saw fit. "Are you quite willing to go to Craiglockhart Hospital?" he asked "Yes", I said, whereupon he replied, "I'm afraid I shall have to send you to the Western General Hospital as Craiglockhart has not the facilities".

I was then shown into a waiting-room where a number of patients were gathered. I was struck by the kindliness and friendliness of the Parish Council staff. They had no difficulty in tracing my pedigree.

Feeling increasingly ill and on the verge of collapse I leaned heavily against one of the other patients for support. Shortly I was conveyed by ambulance to the Western General Hospital and put into a casualty ward where I was exanimed by a coloured doctor with a nurse in attendance, Afterwards I was taken upstairs in a lift and given a wash-down and weighed. If I remember right I was seven stone. I was put into the diabetic ward. My bed was near the window and as I lay there surrounded by patients, I felt utterly contented, all sense of feeling was gone. I was dead and yet not dead. All through the night a nurse sat by my bedside. Sometime in the early hours of the morning I grew restless, the nurse soothed me, the fatigue of my mind and body began to abate. One morning I was conscious of a cool hand on my brow in which there was strength and new vitality was flowing through my veins so that I felt stronger as though been invigorated by the presence of the doctor and matron who bent over me with a sparkle in their eyes but underneath flowed a deep stream of purpose to do good to their fellow creatures and assist them in their hour of need. According to Professor Murray Lyon I was a miracle. "I did not expect you to live", he said, "by all natural laws you should be dead".

116

Prof. Murray Lyon is a brother-in-law of the late Dr. MacLeod, Church Street, Inverness. Through the shades of the evening I could glimpse Edinburgh Castle illuminated against the faint star-dust of the sky, its effect like stage scenery. I was drawing in life and feeling better. Later on there was word of my being removed with a number of other patients to a convalescent home to recuperate. As I refused to go they had no option but to send me to the Eastern General Hospital. After a fortnight there I began to grow restless and pleaded with the house doctor to be allowed to leave. With a somewhat troubled expression on his face he begged me to stay a little while longer as my health was not quite up to standard, but, seeing I was worried, with great reluctance he gave his consent. Outside I hailed a taxi and drove to a house in Stafford Street where I was to collect my belongings which had been retrieved for me by Miss Russell and left there until called for. I did not pay off the taxi, intending to go to the station. As I mounted the steps and rang the bell the door was opened by a woman. I explained my mission whereupon she asked me to come in. My mistrust of people was too deep-rooted so I said, "If you don't mind I would prefer to wait outside". She was most discourteous and her tone seemed unfriendly. "You won't get your things if you don't come in", she said. Her words had a most alarming effect and, warned by some inner compulsion, I began to edge away whereupon she signalled to the taxi man to force me in. I jumped nimbly to one side and evaded him. Scuttling off, like a street vagrant with no fixed abode, I drifted through the crowd. I hurried along to Drumsheugh Gardens and was just in the nick of time for Miss Archibald was about to leave on a long vacation. I explained what had happened and she immediately fetched her car and retrieved my belongings. Then my friend invited me to lunch at MacVitie's in Princes Street. I wasn't feeling hungry but the stimulation of her company gave me an appetite. Afterwards she drove me around and showed me places of interest. During our conversation the little Mission

House was mentioned. Miss Archibald informed me she called to enquire why it was that they had put me into that house in the High Street. She was told not knowing anything about me that they thought it was their duty to 'phone the said place, who informed them what to do. So you see, my suspicions were not unfounded. Suddenly my friend turned the car and drove to the station where she bought me a railway ticket and saw me safely into my compartment. She clasped my hand, kissed me and wished me all the best. At the blast of the whistle the train jerked forward amidst some cries, lurchings and tramplings in the corridor.

Standing on the platform she waved me good-bye as the train steamed out of Waverly Station for Inverness.

CHAPTER 43

ARRIVING AT my destination I went direct to a Mrs Simpson, Three Manse Place, where I stayed a week. I got in touch with Provost MacKenzie of St Andrew's Cathedral who found accommodation for me in the YWCA on Island Bank Road. After a fortnight there I was transferred to Nairn Convalescent Home, for the day, hence to the Nairn Workhouse for the weekend as the poor authorities were paying my fare down to St Mary's Convalescent Home, Thorpe, Chertsey, Surrey, England.

On the morning of my departure (3rd September, 1937) Provost and Mrs MacKenzie and her sister, Mrs MacLeod, motored from Inverness to see me off. At Kings Cross Station, London, I was met by Miss Russell the welfare worker whom I already met in Edinburgh who accompanied me the rest of the journey to the Convalescent Home where I was to stay for an indefinite period. We breakfasted in the Station Hotel. During my convalescence, I was introduced to one of the many great statesmen of our country, Mr George Lansbury, MP, who was opening a sale of work in the grounds.

118

The street urchin felt highly honoured shaking hands with a Member of Parliament. As the weeks went by my health improved and I grew stronger and I went for long walks with some of the other patients and had our tea in the 'Old Mill Inn' with its oak beams overhead, oak tables, each with a lighted candle, and a roaring log fire with copper and brass pots and kettles all decked around. We were given a Devonshire tea, everything home baked. One of the staff took us into Staines one day. Windsor Castle being closed we paid a visit to Windsor Chapel. At Christmas we had a nativity play and I was the beggar sitting on the chancel steps begging from the people who trudged from afar off up to Jerusalem to pay their taxes. Among them were Mary and Joseph. by now the Inn was full and there was no room for them so I stood up and directed them to the stable. The Reverend Mr Finch said, "You made a very good beggar". He has long since passed on.

After eight months I grew restless and longed to return to my native country, Bonnie Scotland. I expressed my desire to seek a light post, the situation was proposed but not accepted. They were under the impression I would make my home there and earn my keep. I began to pine and take fits of weeping and let something of my past experience slip out, of which they had been completely ignorant. Thinking I was slightly mental they motored me down to Woking Mental Hospital. On being examined there was found to be an absence of mental illness, they were fuming at having to take me back. Not satisfied, a local official was brought in who was curious to know the date and place of my birth but I refused to answer. Before long I was put through a third degree which almost drained my life-stream. Coming in one day I was summoned by one of the staff into a waiting room. On entering I was met by two mentally defectives, a shiver ran through me and a faint trickle of fear went coursing down my spine as one of them stuck his face close to mine but, through the 'Grace of Almighty God' I stood my ground, while their orderly stood in the background viewing the scene to see what effect it would have on me. "A criminal offence, punishable by law". He tried to force me to say I was mental but I just kept on saying I am not mental. Noticing his patients were becoming restless he humoured them. Evidently one of them thought he was a doctor for the orderly kept on saying to him, "And what do you think doctor?" Then quite suddenly they left the room, I found myself alone, my legs trembled and I collapsed into a chair. As God is my witness I swear that I have written the truth for truth never changes. I seemed to have a talent for getting myself into difficulties wherever I went. A few days later I was given a strong sedative which put me to sleep.

CHAPTER 44

I CAME up at length out of a great gulf of darkness and found myself in a room in a Nursing Home on Sunbury-on-Thames surrounded by rows of iron beds with other unwanted occupants. Everywhere was silence and the atmosphere was electric. Suddenly it was broken by the most piercing, heart-rendering shrieks, the cries coming in total silence alarmed me. My mind was in a turmoil of bewilderment. I realised this was no ordinary house. Some were drug addicts with that wild dreadful glitter in their eyes, the light of craving for their drugs. The whole place reeked of the vile smell, the small fitted windows being closed. It was torture and I was almost suffocated for the want of air. There were others gazing with a vacant stare in their eyes, sometimes one broke out into excessive fits of laughter, one old woman was seventy years of age and had her hands tied. Woe betide anyone nearby, she would let out with her feet and then start to cackle. After a week I was allowed to rise but was still cooped up in the ward. When going to the toilet I observed the narrowness of the corridors. One day I heard the matron, a Mrs Blamey, who has long since passed on, who was the owner of the nursing Home, say to her assistant, "Nothing has happened yet, I wish something would happen soon, we could make use of her". That was something no one was to hear but me. After a week went by I was allowed to come downstairs to the sitting room where a number of patients were gathered; one took fits of playing the piano then all of a sudden she would stop, into her eyes would come that vacant stare; another thought she was the Queen and insisted on being called 'Her Royal Highness'. My heart went out to them wishing I could free them from their bondage. Before long I had a visit from the doctor who looked at me with ironic amusement in his eyes. (A doctor can turn his skill to taking life or saving it.) I felt the world was going mad and I was going mad as well. (Sooner or later a cat tires of its game.)

One afternoon I collapsed and was bundled off with my few belongings to the Middlesex Hospital. After a week there from the doctors report, there was nothing the matter with me. I asked to be allowed to leave and permission was granted, the Matron gave me a half crown, so after breakfast I took leave. But, where was I to go? I wandered aimlessly around and landed down in Twickenham. My cases were becoming lumbersome and people stared at me curiously as I trudged footsore and weary through the little town, famous for its rugby and football matches.

Somewhere on the outskirts I rested on a grassy bank and down below a river flowed past. I was beginning to feel hungry and a little faint for it was well into the afternoon. So I moved on, going through life without an anchorage with no real hope for the future. Nearby was a Church, I called at the vicarage and begged for food. I was taken in by the clergyman's wife. On leaving I was given seven shillings and sixpence. I then journeyed by bus back to Sunbury. My footsteps led me to the Nursing Home and on ringing the bell the door was opened by a man-servant. Almost simultaneously Mrs

Blamey came into view discreetly gowned. On seeing me she stiffened and before I could speak she demanded to know who let me out of Hospital. I said, "From the Doctor's medical point of view there was nothing the matter with me. I was hoping you would perhaps help me to get back to Aberdeen."

Some people are easily put out of tune by the slightest change of atmosphere. Leaving me standing in the front hall she went to the 'phone, I heard her speaking in low business-like tones; I felt very much on edge and smelt danger and sprang into swift action. Opening the door, I bolted into the rain-swept night, nearly skidding as I turned the corner, and was swallowed up in the darkness.

I made my way up the narrow street and went to the vicarage there thinking the Clergyman would help me. The door was opened by his wife who informed me that her husband was out but was expected in at any moment if I cared to wait. Going in I was given a meal, beside me a baby in a cot cooed lustily. It was between the hours of ten and eleven o'clock at night when the vicar returned. He gave me an address of a house in Richmond Road, Kingston. Handing me some money he directed me to the bus stance. On the way I asked the conductor to let me off at my destination, after which I continued to gaze through the rain spattered windows.

Arriving, I had no difficulty finding the place. A young woman answered the door, her manner was quite respectful as she stood aside to allow me to enter. Evidently they were expecting me because no questions were asked. I was shown my bedroom where there were three empty beds. I was about to undress when my eyes fell on printed matter hanging on the walls. Feeling somewhat curious, I moved closer. I blinked, startled at what I read. There were rules and regulations laid down and the times when to feed babies. I realised this was no ordinary house, I lost no time, the fuse was already lighted. My shoes in my hand, I opened the door, tense and sweating, I crept down the dimly lit stair hardly daring to breathe using

122

my sense of observation. I noticed something like a draught excluder at the foot of the door, also a sneck, and cunningly I clicked up the draught excluder, undid the latch, gently opened the door and tiptoed out. I pulled open the iron-spiked gate, which creaked more than a little, and made good my escape which I hoped would not be discovered immediately. Like a vagrant I sheltered in Kingston Station on a branch line. There was no one about so I lay down on a wooden bench with a canopy of carpeted stars above me; I wearily closed my eyes until the first hint of morning was beginning to lighten the sky. I journeyed back by train to Sunbury-on-Thames. Thinking I was doing the right thing, I went to the Vicarage with the intention of letting the Clergyman know to what sort of place he had sent me. As I approached, he was working in the garden, hearing the sound of my feet on the gravel he turned round, straightened himself to his full height and glared at me. Before I could open my mouth to explain he ordered me off his premises in an authoritative manner, shouting, "Get away from here or I'll send the Police to you". No doubt he meant well, but thought I was an incurable vagrant. Stunned and bewildered at being denied human aid I covered my face with my hands and ran blindly away, picking up my luggage at the gate and stumbled down the road. On the brink of despair, from the depths of my being. I cried out in agony, "Dear Lord, what am I to do? Nobody cares, nobody wants me, where shall I go, to whom shall I go?" Tears streamed down my face.

My breathless run slowed to a walk when a Policeman on a bicycle appeared on the scene and, without my knowledge, my footsteps were directed to the Police Box where the Arm of the Law shared with me half of his lunch and a cup of coffee. Shortly the Police car came and drove me to the Middlesex Institution. There I made known to the Governor that I wished to return to Aberdeen and asked his co-operation. He replied, "I'll see if it can be arranged". As the days slipped by my chances of going to Aberdeen became no more definite.

I grew weary, for every time I broached the subject I was put off with strange evasive answers. At last growing desperate, I dared myself to go to his office and explained if he couldn't help me I was leaving. He admitted I couldn't be kept against my will so I packed my few belongings and walked out. No one stood in my way, I was free to go. Years later I was sorry to learn that the clergyman's child had died, and that he too had passed on.

CHAPTER 45

NOT FAR away was a second-hand dealer's shop. To try and raise some money I slipped a nine carat gold heart shaped engraved pendant off my neck and went in and gave it to the dealer. On examining it he shook his head and handed it back. Then, all of a sudden, he asked me through to his back room, feeling scared I backed out and fled, breaking my heart, weeping. I wandered around for a while then again went to a nearby vicarage. The housekeeper took me in and gave me a meal. While I was eating a name flashed across my mind I heard spoken of in St. Margaret's Convent, Aberdeen. Thanking the housekeeper I took leave and boarded a bus up to London and came off somewhere near Marble Arch and enquired of a passer-by where I could get a bus for East Grinstead, Sussex. The person to whom I spoke was an Irishman out of work, living in digs in Bayswater Road. He kindly accompanied me to the bus stop in Park Lane, carrying my case the short distance. Counting my money, to my dismay, I realised I hadn't enough money to pay my fare. Looking around I noticed a Minister standing on the other side of Park Lane. Once again I did not relish the thought of having to beg in the streets. Going over I stood alongside of him and made some remark about the weather and then said, "I wonder if you could please help me with my fare down to East Grinstead", showing him what silver I had in my wee purse. He smiled a little and handed me some money and all this time his wife stood by watching. "I thought that was coming", she exclaimed, her words dampened my spirits but I looked up into the eyes of the Minister and thanked him. Crossing over to the bus stop my eyes lighted on a little green painted door with a brass knob, it was the back entrance to Twenty-nine Norfolk Street, Park Lane, S.W.1. Casting my mind back, I remembered my three years with the Sedge-wicks it was I who kept the little brass knob clean. The screech-ing of the bus brought me to earth and I got inside. I reached East Grinstead dead beat and staggered along to St. Margaret's in Moat Road, which is the Mother House of St. Margaret's Convent, Seventeen Spital, Aberdeen, to be told there was no room for me. ('There was no room at the Inn'.) However, they very kindly gave me an address of a Welfare Worker, a Miss Perkins, who lived nearby in Moat Road.

On reaching her house I discovered there was nobody at home. I called next door and enquired and was informed that Miss Perkins was on holiday and that her sister who kept house was out for the evening and wouldn't be back till late. "Oh thank you very much", I said and turned away. I felt so tired and could hardly hold my head up. I looked around for somewhere to rest and going into a woodshed I sank on the floor, overcome by weakness and weariness. I was twenty-eight years of age and the future was very bleak for me, for the view was blotted out by mist. I belonged to a world of forgottens and, as I lay crumpled up in a corner, my heart turned sick at the thought, dreading the swift passage of time, nothing mattered any more. The sound of footsteps reached my ears then suddenly the squeaking of the shed door as it was slowly pushed open. A woman appeared, it was the neighbour I had spoken to in the earlier part of the evening. "You must be tired", she murmured sympathetically and helped me to my feet and escorted me into her house and seated me by the fireside while she prepared a hot stimu-lant. A Westminster clock on the mantlepiece chimed out half past twelve, I felt like the dark midnight for I did not know what the morning would bring. My memory flashed back to the Dean Village when, as a child, I was left out clinging to the railings, my sobs drowned in the surging waters of the River Dean. A neighbour would come and take me in and seat me by her fireside with a hot glass of milk in my hand. My hostess left me for a few moments. Suddenly I heard voices, the good lady of the house appeared with Miss Perkins whose presence was like a breath of fresh air. Somehow I felt a gleam of hope surge through me, my mind found contact with someone who understood me. She was tall and slender and fair of face and had clear blue eyes, her healthy bloom gave her a cheerful appearance. She kindly thanked her neighbour for looking after me. Taking my arm she piloted me into her home then I gave her a brief outline of what had befallen me. She explained to me that her sister was on holiday but she would do all she could to help find me work. Miss Perkins showed me to my bedroom and made down the bed, putting a hot water bottle in, wished me a good night's rest and told me not to worry. In the morning we breakfasted together then called on a Mrs Williams who kept a Domestic Agency in Queen Street, she was a motherly old soul whose husband was a Postman. Fortune smiled on me for that very day I had an interview with a lady out at Crawley Down Lodge. Before I left she said to her house-keeper, "Give her a good meal, to me she looks half starved", which was unhappily true.

The next day, being the month of May, 1938, I was installed as a single-handed table maid in the home of Mr and Mrs Bradshaw, Crawley Down Lodge, Crawley Down, East Grinstead, Sussex. Mr Bradshaw was chief Director of the Midland Bank, London. My wages were fifteen shillings a week plus insurance stamps and laundry money. Some weeks later on one of my frequent visits to the home of Mrs Williams she mentioned that Miss Perkins, the Welfare Worker, when speaking to her at the agency one day passed the remark that if she had been at home when I came on the scene she would have packed me off back to Edinburgh. In due course I understand she regretted her hastily spoken words. So after four months I gave in my notice which seemed rather unkind but Mr and Mrs Bradshaw knew my heart was set on returning to Aberdeen and to look for a light post, also clear up some unfinished business concerning my visit to Marischal College in the year 1934.

CHAPTER 46

ON THE morning of my departure Miss Perkins arrived at Crawley Down Lodge with her car and drove me to her private residence in Moat Road where I spent the night. Next day, Saturday, the two Misses Perkins accompanied me up to London and saw me safely aboard the 'Aberdonian'. As the berths were all booked sleeping quarters were found for me in the hold of the ship. My friends stood on the Lime Wharf Quay and waved good-bye as the ship sailed out with the seven o'clock tide on the last day of August 1938, bound for Aberdeen. As I stood on the deck gazing out to sea I could hardly believe I was under way, leaving behind me a vivid and frightening memory of unfortunate incidents which took place within the first ten months of my stay in England. At last the long looked for day arrived, my body glowed and my veins tingled as I glimpsed the faint outlines of Aberdeen. Wisps of white cloud floated high above as the 'Aberdonian' dropped anchor in Matheson's Quay at nine o'clock on Monday morning.

Fishing boats and harbour wall and the usual panorama of industrialism met me when I stepped ashore, where all was aglow and the cry of the sea gulls heralding in another day in the history of my life. Suffering slightly from the effects of past experience, I was still very much on edge and saw danger where none existed though I fought grimly against my fears.

I made my way to the house of Bethany in the Hardgate who ran a small guest house and there I stayed till I got my bearings. After a few weeks rest I signed on to my former physician, Doctor Frank Milne Rorie, MB, Ch.B, Albyn Place. His great sense of humour helped to bring back my sense of balance. I knew him to be a man of courage and independence of mind and a real benefactor of mankind. Doctor Rorie died on the 16th December, 1949.

> *"For Friendship hath the skill and observation of*
>   *the best physician,*
> *The diligence and vigilance of the best nurse,*
> *And the tenderness and patience of the best Mother"*
>   *Lord Claredon*

> *"A faithful friend is better than gold, medicine for*
>   *misery, an only possession"*
>
>   *Burton*

> *"We are most of us very lonely in this World, you*
>   *who have any who love you, cling to them and*
>   *thank God"*   *W. M. Thackeray*

I also paid a visit to Marischal College to speak with Professor Rex Knight and to learn the reason of my previous visit in the year 1934 and was told I had nothing to fear as I had out-grown my childishness and had greatly advanced in development. The Professor was well acquainted with my life history and had given me every encouragement to write my Autobiography. He was then teaching in King's College. The little experience I had in the Nursing Home run by a highly efficient staff enhanced my education. I had not long to wait before I was offered the post as companion to an invalid lady in Grosvenor Place which lasted three months. I learned from a relative that Miss Duckiet had already two operations for cancer in Kepplestone Nursing Home some time ago. There were times when she would be very sick and vomit which looked like black coffee grounds, also complaining of a sore head which kept her from sleeping. This evening she asked me to look at her head so I sat her down on a stool in front of the coal fire and put a towel round her shoulders and with a comb I parted the hair gently at the back of the ears. I felt the blood drain away from my face at what I saw, it was all the world like an ant's nest, scrambling over one another. Suddenly she turned and looked up at my face, "What's wrong Elizabeth?" "Och it's nothing", I said, "I will soon have you cleaned up in no time". As soon as they fell on the towel and the floor they immediately died. I took a sample to Doctor Frank Rorie, he let me have a look at them through his microscope, they were reddish in colour with little legs. No wonder she couldn't sleep at nights. Next day I made an appointment with Pat Grant, the hairdresser, to have her hair shaved off. When she came home she made a joke of it, smiling she said, "Look, that's all they have left me with, a tufty of hair in the front". The hairdresser gave her some antiseptic ointment to rub on her scalp as it was badly marked. She had a good night's sleep after that. A week later she took a bad turn, I sent for Doctor Richardson. After he had examined her I gave her a bed bath. Next day Miss Duckiet was taken by ambulance to the Armstrong Nursing Home, Albyn Place, where she had a private room and a coal fire. I went to the Nursing Home every day and sat beside her. She would say to me, "If I fall asleep waken me up and take me home". Mr Mitchell, the Surgeon, said she was beyond human aid — six weeks later she died. Her remains were brought home to Grosvenor Place on the Saturday where she lay in state till Tuesday. Alone in the house the atmosphere was eerie and gave me the creeps, I also had a touch of the flu which didn't help any. The day of the funeral, the service was held in the house. Mr Reith, St

Ninian's Church, shook hands with me and smiling a little said, "I was with Miss Duckiet before she died and she asked me to thank you for making her last days happy".

I then rented a furnished room in ninety A Chapel Street from a Mrs MacKie. My first night in the house I was awakened in the early hours of the morning by her husband who seemed to be in great distress as his wife had taken ill. I hastily dressed myself and nursed her through the weary hours of suffering. She was very much discoloured and I had to coax her gently all the time for she kept on trying to get out of bed. Doctor Elizabeth Walker visited her daily. A week later while I was sitting by her bedside she slipped quietly away. I took the pillow from under her head, closed her eyes and mouth. When Doctor Walker came she asked if I would wash her, which I did, and laid her out ready for the undertaker. Mrs MacKie died of cancer in the left breast.

CHAPTER 47

MY NEXT post was companion to a Miss Craig, a retired school teacher, two hundred and forty-nine Queens Road. Doctor Rorie, Albyn Place, and Sister Caroline, St Margaret's Convent, seventeen Spital, Old Aberdeen, spoke for me. Miss Craig was a lady of culture and breeding, with a motherly face and a quick and charming smile who did all in her power to make me happy and feel at home, lavishing all her affections on me. Yes, I was very happy, almost carefree, but deep down in the recesses of my mind there was always the fear it wouldn't last. I had just been three years with her when she took a stroke. Doctor Lady Mary Esslemont attended her daily. A trained nurse was called in from the Northern Nursing Home, Albyn Place, to do night duty, and a relative came in to help during the daytime while I coped with the daily chores, also helped with the nursing. Miss Craig died in February 1942 leaving a roof over my head and a little money. For the second time since Auntie Barbara died in August 1936 I felt a feeling of security. Later on I made arrangements with Miss Craig's lawyers, Edmonds and Ledingham, Golden Square, to sell the house as it took too much to keep up. I then set up house in a tenement, September 3rd, 1942. The first morning I woke up in my own home I was like a child with a new toy. I thanked my Divine Creator, the giver of all good things. Soon I settled down and made a few friends locally who invited me to their homes and they in return visited me. My favourite haunts were along the lower Deeside road, also a round about bus tour by-passing the little town of Ballater, and Braemar, world famous where once a year the gathering of the clans in all their magnificent glory of ancient history muster in great strength to the skirl of the bagpipes to display their valour and skill in a record of exciting athletic events and piping contests. The bus stopped for a few minutes to glimpse at the inside of Crathie Church. In the distance Dark Loch-na-Gar of great height looking like a fortress heavily fortified on all sides ever ready to do or die for this land and its inhabitants and where Balmoral Castle nestles amidst idyllic scenery which wears the look of peace and quiet, harmonising with the lovely wooded slopes and wild tangle of woods and lonely moors, where the Royal Family enjoy the finest of Scottish sports, well named Royal Deeside.

EPILOGUE

In the year 1953, I felt a sudden impulse and urge to write about myself recalling to my mind a record of events and happenings. The interest Professor Rex Knight showed in my well-being inspired me. So, little by little, I began to weave the framework and structure and gradually piece it together; halfway through I started to take writers' cramp and began to feel sick and tired and vowed I never wanted to see paper and pencil again. I took the manuscript page by page and burnt it. Then I got in touch with the Professor at Kings College and told him what I had done, his extraordinary answer took me completely by surprise, for he said, "Never mind Lizzie, in six weeks' time you will be writing again". Sure enough without a doubt I saw myself scrambling out of bed at two o'clock in the early hours of the morning to search for paper and pencil and not forgetting the rubber, In 1955 the tenement I lived in changed hands and was to be turned into a boarding house so I made tracks for the Highland capital and finished the story. I am indebted to Kenneth MacRae (Coinneach Mor) journalist and author, also to his father the Reverend Mr MacRae for correcting and enhancing the manuscript. In 1976 I wrote it over again for in my enthusiasm I had left out vital information here and there.

So end the wanderings of a discarded brat. I wish the proceeds of this book to go to charity.

Elizabeth McKay
6th June, 1977